Blue Remembered Hills

Blue Remembered Hills

A Radnorshire Journey

by
James Roose-Evans

PORT MEADOW PRESS

Port Meadow Press
43 Leckford Road, Oxford OX2 6HY
Registered Co. No. 4405635

ISBN 978-1-9998379-9-0

In loving memory of Hywel Jones
who treasured Bleddfa
and gave so much

Introduction

As a boy of nine or ten I used to sit in the window seat on the first floor landing of my grandfather's house in the Forest of Dean, and gaze at the Black Mountains in the distance. They weren't always black, but mostly as mauve and blue as Housman's "blue remembered hills". Beyond them lay another country called Wales, which for me was as wrapped in mystery as the mountains often were in mist. It was a land where people spoke a different language, played harps and, so I was told, sang like angels! Little did I know that one day I would have a home in Wales and even begin to speak the language. What I did know was that my paternal grandmother was a Miss Rhoose from Rhyll, and that my paternal grandfather, the Reverend Owen Morgan was from Monmouth.

For more than fifty years I have kept a journal. When it was suggested that I should draw together some of the material in book form it was with the idea of evoking a sense of place: the landscape, its people and a quality of life in the Welsh Borders that remains largely unspoilt to this day. In the process of editing, rearranging, shaping and rewriting I came to see that this was also a story about a spiritual journey into the unknown.

Recently I came across the phrase, "Leap – and the net will appear", and it seems to me that I have been doing this all my life; whether it was in starting the Hampstead Theatre in London with no previous experience of running a theatre and no financial backing, or founding the Bleddfa Centre for the Creative Spirit. Certainly, in going to live in a small community in Wales and becoming involved with the village church and school, I had no idea that I would also be setting out on the path towards becoming a priest …

One day at breakfast, my mother made an announcement:

"Your father and I are going to live together again," (they had separated in the 1950s.)

"Is that sensible?" I asked, remembering her fear of my father, especially when drunk.

"Oh, we are older and wiser now," she replied. "After all, we are both in our seventies."

And that is how the story begins …

1970

Hywel and I visit a property in Radnorshire, on the borders of Wales, which my mother has located. It is the Old Rectory – in a tiny hamlet called Bleddfa.

The name in Welsh means "place of the wolves". It is said that wolves roamed wild in this area right up until Tudor times. Throughout the Middle Ages Bleddfa remained an isolated Lordship, the only Welsh possession of a Herefordshire estate based at Richard's Castle, near Ludlow. A castle was built here in the twelfth century and a royal grant given to repair it in 1195, but it was not rebuilt after the Welsh prince Llywelyn ap Gruffydd destroyed it in 1262. Only the mound on which it once stood remains. In 1402 Owain Glyndwr's rebel army won a dramatic and famous victory at Pilleth, close by to the East, against the English army of Sir Edmund Mortimer. Shortly before, during the rising of 1401–2, parts of Bleddfa itself, including the church tower, are said to have been put to the torch by Glyndwr's men. Nothing much of national significance seems to have happened in the following centuries. The first set of traffic lights was installed in Radnorshire in the year 2000!

Bleddfa is a hamlet – not even a village. Its main buildings are a small post-office-cum-shop, a small school, the

Hundred House Inn, which, until 1867 doubled-up as the courthouse, and a fine medieval church. But Bleddfa does have its own poet, the Reverend Samuel Phillips, who was born in 1754 in Cwmygerwin, half a mile away, baptised and married in Bleddfa church, and who now lies buried in its churchyard along with his wife, Elizabeth Moore of Newtown, Montgomeryshire, and their baby son, Samuel, who died on November 14th 1777, just a few days after his baptism. The Reverend Samuel left behind him a collection of poems, written in his own hand, including this Epitaph for an Old Maid:

Scorning and Scorn'd, she passed her life away,
An useless lump of animated Clay;
Now Spite and Envy rule her frame no more,
But here it lies – more useless than before!

SEPTEMBER 10TH

The Old Rectory, hidden behind tall trees, stands next to the thirteenth century church of St Mary Magdalene. It has been newly wired and decorated by a builder who wants a quick sale. There is still rubble in the cellar, as well as a toad, and a bat, which opens one eye in the beam of my torch.

From the enclosed garden, a small side gate leads into the churchyard. "Your father and I won't have far to go when our time comes," observes my mother.

Although I suspect woodworm in the attic, the house feels so right that I insist on driving at once to the estate agent and putting down a deposit without even bothering to arrange a surveyor's report. £6,500. I have only £2,000 in the bank, but various friends have said they are willing to loan the rest.

SEPTEMBER 12TH

It is market day in Knighton, and the small town is full of farmers and their wives in their best dresses and hats, gathered in small groups up and down the one steep street, chattering away like starlings. Everyone's cheeks are glowing, buffed by the wind as though rouged.

We take coffee in Hall's. Mr Hall is the town's baker and undertaker. In the front of the shop he bakes bread and in the back he makes coffins. Once, in the small hours of the morning, one of his young assistants was startled to hear a ticking from within a newly arrived coffin. When the lid was opened it was discovered that the sound was emanating from the dead man's hearing aids!

We listen to the women talking at the next table. Underneath the surface of their conversation you sense the aching nerve of hardship as well as the loneliness of isolation on some of the outlying farms, especially where the wives have not learned to drive.

"Last night I slept so deep. I haven't slept like that for months. I don't get out much."

"I only had two hours sleep last night. If only I could get rid of this pain in my knee. I get up and make tea and take an aspirin, but I wish they could find a cure for this arthritis."

Another describes the difficulties of looking after her aged father on the hill farm.

It is difficult for those who live in urban areas to imagine the bleak conditions under which many country people still live. I hear from a local doctor how one night he was called out to an isolated hill farm where the old farmer had just died. His wife was sitting by the fire when he arrived in the small hours. "He's up there!" she indicated, pointing to the stairs.

He found her husband lying in the brass bed and when he came downstairs, having certified that the old man was indeed dead, all his wife said was, "Better shut the door, Doctor, else the dog will be at him!" Listening to this story I was reminded of R.S. Thomas' poem about his visit, as Rector, to one of his country parishioners who had recently died, and his discovery of the man lying "on the vast and lonely shore of that bleak bed".

Walking up the street we come to Rudge's, the butcher's shop. On either side of the door are two large hooks, suspended from which is the carcass of a pig, slung up by its trotters, its nose dripping blood onto the pavement. Mr Rudge is in the process of sawing the carcass from the top downwards, from tail to neck, so that the two halves begin to curve. Then, taking a cleaver, with two swift blows he chops the head precisely in two so that from each hook there hangs half a pig. It is at this point that the small crowd of customers waiting to enter pass in between the two halves of the pig and begin to make their purchases.

SEPTEMBER 28ᵀᴴ

I return to Bleddfa to find the house reeking of Rentokil, with many of the wooden floors covered in polythene sheets. I stay overnight at the Hundred House Inn and awake the next morning to find the valley thick with mist, and the cries of a farmer on the side of the hill rounding up sheep, calling to his dog, "Hep! Hep! Good boy!" and the excited yelps of the collie in response.

Suddenly there is the chatter of young voices and, looking out of the window, I can see several small children getting out of a local taxi. Shortly afterwards the school bell tolls and the children all file into the one-room building for their lessons.

SEPTEMBER 29ᵀᴴ

The removal men arrive and I supervise my mother's furniture and chattels being distributed to different rooms. I get a lift into Llandrindod Wells, where I bump into the playwright Donald Howarth, whose *Lily in Little India* was first staged at the Hampstead Theatre Club. I discover that he lives near Builth Wells and he encourages me to go with him to a local auction where I buy a hundred books for a pound, two bedpans and a large washing basin for one shilling, a glass and mahogany Cadbury's chocolate display cabinet for three pounds and an old chamber pot. "You can use that," says Donald, "to serve potatoes in!"

His car is piled with books and he has to disgorge a magpie's nest of tools, empty bottles and junk from the boot to make room for my display cabinet. Even so, we have to drive back to the Old Rectory with the boot open. When I eventually come to cook potatoes – and serve them in the pot – they taste of urine!

OCTOBER 10TH

My father returns from America and the old rows resume as he gets increasingly drunk and threatening. "I am not stupid, you know!" he rants. "I know I'm not wanted here. I'm just a labourer; the lowest of the low is what your mother calls me."

OCTOBER 11TH

I get up at six thirty as I have to go back to London. As I open my bedroom door Mother opens hers and giggles as she whispers for us to be quiet. I switch off the light in the kitchen in case my father, sleeping in the room above, should see its reflection. I shave by torch and then sit with mother in candlelight, whispering. Through the window I can see clouds racing past the moon. "It's awful to whisper!" says Mother, and I reply, "But fun!"

I set out to walk the eight or so miles to Knighton to catch the train. Looking back along the valley, the hills are already covered with snow, and as cottages and farmhouses switch on their lights it is as though stars have fallen to earth. Trucks pass me but none stop. Then, after walking two miles, a car pulls up to offer me a lift. The driver tells me that the worst snows come at the end of January and can last through February. The other occupants of the car are two silent, sleepy young women whom he drops off at the trouser factory on the outskirts of Knighton. I walk through the darkened town. In the butcher's shop youths in blue and white striped aprons are cutting up the carcasses. There is the smell of baking bread coming from Hall's; but the only shop open is the newsagent's, selling the morning papers and cigarettes.

NOVEMBER 20TH

My mother has collapsed. I send for the local doctor, Brian Davies, who has, I have been warned, a reputation for plain speaking. He examines her and then takes me to one side. "There's only one thing wrong with your mother," he says, "and that's your father!"

And so I have to break it to my father that he should go back to America. "It's no one's fault," I say. "It's simply that you and mother just don't get on – so it is better you should live apart." He decides to leave the next morning and spend Christmas with friends in England before returning to America.

DECEMBER 14TH

I find Mr Powell, seated in his car outside. He lives up the lane in a bungalow. He has a bad stammer and I wait patiently while he tells me he has been shopping in Knighton and it has been raining. "But I had my humber – my humber – I had my humberella!"

I ask if I may call on him one day and have a chat, and which is best, morning or afternoon? "Oh, afternoon!"

he replies. "We aren't too good in the morning. My wife isn't well and I haven't been too well either. It's the pains in my s-s-stomach. I've had them for years. I thought w-w-walking would be good for it, but sitting still is best. I s-s-sit in my chair and take s-s-some powders."

I later learn that he went to school as a boy in Bleddfa, has lived in the area all his life, and didn't marry until he was fifty. One day a fellow pupil from the school, Ron Watkins, who had gone to work for ICI and travelled the world, came back for a visit. Crossing a field he encountered Mr Powell on horseback. They greeted one another and Mr Powell, looking down from his horse, asked, "Where be working now, Ron?" to which he replied, "Birmingham". To Mr Powell, who had never travelled more than fifty miles away, this was beyond his comprehension. There was a pause. Then he asked, "And how many acres be Birmingham?"

DECEMBER 16TH

I follow the hill track up and over to the next village of Llangunllo. The moon is full, with Orion lying low on the skyline. The higher one climbs the more the countryside seems to tilt. Owls hoot, bats cry, and there is the occasional squeak of a shrew being caught. I hear the put-put-put of an electricity generator from an upland farm. Occasionally the moon breaks through the clouds and then the fields shine white and the sheep move slowly like ghostly visitants. Up here, between the two villages, it seems wilder and more remote, so that on a night like this it is easy to imagine Owain Glyndwr massing his troops for the assault on Mortimer's men and the ensuing massacre at Pilleth where, as the old chronicles relate, "the Welsh women committed atrocities upon the bodies of the slaughtered English" – which I take to mean that they cut off their genitals.

DECEMBER 18TH

Mother tells me that she recently walked up the lane as far as the last farmhouse and, meeting the old farmer who lived there, she asked him, "Where does this lane lead?"

He replied, "You just go on and on and you come to Heaven!"

"Well," said my mother, "that sounds like an easy way of getting there. Next time I'm out I'll see how far I get and let you know."

"Ah!" he answered. "There's no-one ever come back to tell us!"

"Perhaps I'll be the first!" laughed my mother. "Like the men on the moon!"

The farmer went on to tell how one day he was out in the fields when the man who used to buy their eggs for market called at the house and happened upon the dead body of his wife. She was sitting bolt upright at her desk, writing out an order. "Well, the chap came to find me and he said, 'Have you seen your wife lately?' So I went home and sure enough found her dead. Now I live alone with my son who spends every evening in the pub playing darts. He parks his tractor right outside your house."

1971

At the Old Rectory I spend a couple of hours digging a two foot trench all round the house, prior to cementing against rising damp. I get a lift into Knighton with a man who tells me that the slowness in local retailers sending their bills goes back to former times when farmhands were paid just once a year at harvest time.

"You see this gear I have on? It's nearly worn out and I've still not had the bill. When I bought this suit, I said to John who runs the men's outfitting shop in Llandrindod, 'How much is it? I'll pay you now.' And John replied, 'It'll be about so-and-so. But the invoices haven't come in yet, so let me send you a bill later.'"

He also tells me that, in Radnorshire, if someone says he'll come to do a job at ten thirty in the morning, it is almost certain he means four in the afternoon. "You soon get used to it!" He reckons children didn't walk such long distances to school in the old days. "If you work it out they'd never have made it in time. But the women used to walk to market, leaving at dawn with their baskets. Made a day of it. And thought nothing of it."

I have now cleared out the cellar. Against one wall is an oak frame supporting a thick slab of slate originally used for salting the hams. I have converted this into an altar, with two candles in iron holders on either side, and against the opposite wall I have placed a pine settle. Inset into the walls on each side, at ground level, are two small apertures for letting in air, through which one can hear the birds in the garden. Here I sit and meditate.

FEBRUARY 10TH

The Rector calls to introduce himself, partly out of curiosity, having discovered that I am writing a weekly article on meditation for *The Church Times*. I am not a churchgoer. For the past fifteen years or so, like countless others, I have moved away from the Church as an institution, no longer finding it nurturing. However, living here in the Old Rectory, next to the village church, it seems that the least I can do whenever I am in residence is to attend the weekly Eucharist. And so, along with an elderly couple, Mr and Mrs Watson, and Brian Williams who works for the Forestry Commission, I swell the congregation to four.

I make my way through the little gate from my garden into the churchyard, following the path that so many in the past must have taken to the church. Inside, I hear the Rector saying to Mrs Watson, "Do you know this hymn? Number 221. We ought to have one about the Saints." The remaining two of the congregation arrive. We stand to sing two hymns. During the second, the tune of which I don't know – and there is no accompaniment – only Mr and Mrs Watson sing, falteringly. I kneel down and bury my head in my hands. Why plough through verse after verse like this? The last stanza is used to cover the Rector's walk from the chancel down the nave to the back of the church so that at the end he can turn round and say, "Let us pray," and then race us through yet another prayer.

As I leave I overhear Mr Watson asking the Rector, "Why didn't Mr Roose-Evans take Communion?"

MARCH 10TH

Evening (just after eleven o'clock). I walk up the lane to investigate a brilliant white light. In the first barn lamps are hung low over a pen made up of hurdles roped together, inside which, nestling in the warmth, three tiny lambs are asleep, while in other pens ewes stand with their lambs at their side. I walk on to the next barn slung across with cables, and lamps suspended from them. The yard is littered with straw, feeding troughs lined up against one wall. Under the dazzling lights the place is a concourse of pregnant ewes, huge and swollen, standing, kneeling, lying. With their white bony faces, tufted ears and thick manes of wool, they resemble a gathering of Dutch aristocrats. The straw muffles all sound. There is a stillness, a sense of waiting. Occasionally one ewe butts another; one sneezes several times; a third gets up from its knees, as though finishing its devotions, and yields its place to another. There is a quiet coming and going like that of worshippers in a Russian Orthodox church. Occasionally there is the baa-ing of a lamb and the deeper lowing of cattle from another barn.

Easter Sunday

The church is festive with branches of laurel and black-thorn, catkins and vases of daffodils. When we arrive, the Rector is kneeling at his desk saying Matins on his own at the top of his voice, oblivious to those trying quietly to pray! In his sermon he talks about our great future and responsibility – while outside there is a ceaseless baa-ing of lambs. I cannot help thinking of Jesus' words "Feed my sheep! Feed my lambs!" and I find myself pondering the role of the priest as pastor to his people.

Our Rector hardly ever visits anyone to ask how they are getting on, not even popping in to see the Baileys, an elderly couple who live in the tiny cottage adjoining the school.

Hywel begins to teach me how to drive. We go to Llandrindod Wells to practise, and discover Pen-y-Bont Common, where George Fox once preached to a great gathering of Quakers. It was because of the persecution of Quakers that so many emigrated from here to Pennsylvania, where today there are towns and villages named after their counterparts in Radnorshire.

We drive on and as we approach Pen-y-Bont we pass a bent old woman carrying a basket, walking with difficulty, her body twisted. It is like a scene from the opening of a Thomas Hardy novel: the bleak expanse of common land, the road stretching away, and this solitary figure.

When later we return from Llandrindod Wells she is still struggling along the road. "I wonder if she would like a lift?" asks Hywel who is now driving. He stops the car and runs back to speak to her. As he is about to help her into the car she winces with pain and snaps, "Let me manage on my own!"

A tiny, fragile figure, twisted with arthritis, she lolls like a child on the back seat. She tells us she was born in 1905 and used to walk three-and-a-half miles to school and back again when she was six. She now walks the four miles to Llandrindod to do her shopping and then the four miles back. She does this every day.

"It's something to do," she adds. We turn off the main road and drive for a mile up a narrow twisting lane.

"Sometimes," she tells us, "I have to climb up the bank to get out of the way – the cars drive so fast."

"What do you do in the winter?" I ask. "Do you still walk to the shops?"

"Oh, I've been up to my legs in snow many a time! But this summer it's been so hot I've had to carry buckets of water up from the farm below. You can stop now. This is it. I'll get out here."

"It" is a small, blue-painted wooden house, looking bare and neglected, perched high on the hillside, over-looking the valley and the road below. She slides slowly and carefully out of the car and then peers up, smiling, to thank us. I help carry her heavy bag into the decaying house. In the main room, where she sleeps in a chair, there is a strong smell of excrement, crumbs everywhere on the flagstones, and plates of food set down for her many cats, one of which has just peed on the floor. There is an old kitchen range heaped with ashes and a lit oil stove with the kettle simmering on it.

"What time did you go out?" I ask.

"Eleven," she replies. It is now three o'clock.

On a chair is a pile of clothes, and on a table unwashed dishes and food. She stands, her head bowed with the arthritis, peering at me quizzically.

"Soon be Whitsun," she says. "It was Whitsun nine years ago my husband died. We'd been to shop, got back, had a cup of tea, and were sitting together when he died. It was such a shock I couldn't even cry."

As we leave, she stands at the door, bidding us be careful as we drive down the lane. She is like a bird with one wing drooping, yet she survives, living alone with her two dozen cats. Her name is Joyce Penfold.

The village shop – even though technically Bleddfa is a hamlet everyone refers to the place as a village – is a small, low-ceilinged room which also serves as a sub post-office, where Jean Thomas and her mother, Ruth Casson, take it in turns to serve, often having to stand and listen patiently to long sagas from their customers. There is a counter, and shelves crowded with mops, packets of Vim and Fairy Liquid, tins of food, packets of crisps, wrapped sliced bread, folders of envelopes and writing paper, Christmas and birthday cards, boxes of chocolates, cigarettes and tobacco, bacon and butter, cheese and vegetables, coloured pencils and children's favourite sweets including jelly beans, Spangles, Mars bars, and Hundreds and Thousands.

"You must come and try some of Mum's beetroot wine!" says Jean one evening, inviting me into their kitchen, where, on the stove, sits a frying pan and in it a mound of tea leaves drying.

"What is that for?" I ask. Ruth reaches up for a round tin, full of dried tea leaves.

"In the spring I mix them and then put the mixture down on the flower beds to kill the slugs."

She also saves coal dust to make briquettes, which she uses when lighting the fire. Like all of us who grew up during the Second World War she has cultivated the art of thrift. Waste not want not!

She is a passionate gardener and, like all gardeners, is a natural philosopher.

"You get no end of disappointments," she observes. "Plants killed by the frost, or seemingly for no reason at all. You can try to grow lots of things and they won't take, and so you learn to do without them, while other things you find can grow and flourish with no trouble at all."

"That's a philosophy for life!" I say.

"Yes, it is!" she replies and gives me a warm embrace.

She describes a walk she took in the bad winter of 1962. By a footbridge over a stream she found a robin with one leg frozen to a gate. Taking hold of it she pulled quickly and the one leg came away, leaving the other still frozen to the gate.

"Then I put him under my sweater and scarves and continued to walk as was my wont. And forgot about him. When I got back here he was chirping away! I fed him and kept him in a cardboard box on top of the grandfather clock and put his food there. At intervals he would fly about the room. And he was like that for a month until one day, when the weather was milder, I opened the kitchen window without thinking, and he flew to join the other birds at the bird table, balancing on his one leg. I saw him for the next day or two and then not again. Other birds are so cruel to maimed creatures and I don't expect he survived."

Later that evening I go down to inscribe the latest of my *Odd and Elsewhere* books for Jean and Albert Thomas's eldest daughter, Beth. Albert comes in from work, his face glowing from the cold outside, rubbing his calloused hands across his eyes. He works for Farmer George and has been hedging. He is a master craftsman at pleating hedges, which is very much a dying art. He and I sit by the fire, talking quietly, while Jean and Ruth cut a large plateful of bread and butter, and cook eggs and chips, which we eat on trays in front of the television.

OCTOBER 20TH

Back from Athens, where I have been directing Sophocles' *Oedipus* with a cast of Greek actors. On my return I call to see Mr and Mrs Bailey who live in the tiny cottage attached to the village school, where the schoolmistress would once have lived. It has just two rooms, one up, one down, no bathroom, and a lean-to scullery at the back which also serves as a kitchen. It reminds me of my boyhood when, on Friday nights, saucepans and kettles would be filled with water to heat and I would sit in an enamel bath in front of the fire.

When I arrive, Mr and Mrs Bailey are sitting in the dark in front of a large fire. "We like to make the most of the gloaming," says Mrs Bailey. "That way we save on electricity."

Mr Bailey recalls Llandrindod Wells in the days of its prosperity, when it was still a spa town for the gentry, who came from London with all their servants on special trains.

"In those days you had to buy a ticket to get on the platform, and when a train came in, the platform would be jammed with people, while outside there'd be hansom cabs waiting to take folk to their hotels.

"Already at five thirty each morning you'd see the streets and pavements being swept and shops setting out their goods on the pavement. Later there'd be people promenading to the park, the lake, and to the spa itself to take the waters. The place would be full of colour and crowds. It's gone through many changes since and Llandod isn't what it used to be in my day. Nowadays, it's a ghost of itself."

The blackened kettle simmers and we have buttered scones and home-made cake, while Mrs Bailey tells me how, forty years ago, hill farmers, travelling down from an upland farm with a coffin on a horse-drawn cart, would sing hymns, "but now it is all dying out".

She talks about her training as a nurse down among the docks in London in the 1920s. "It took twenty minutes to blanket-wash a patient. And once I saw someone having their leg sawn off as though it were a log, and then the arteries all tied up, the skin folded and stitched in place."

Her sister, who was also a nurse, died of cancer because the doctor never bothered about an X-ray until it was too late.

"Today, of course, anaesthetics have improved, but in the old days you had to be standing by when a patient came round in case he suffocated on his own vomit."

They tell me about the cottage they once had up in the hills outside Ludlow, near the Devil's Chair. In half an hour you could be in Ludlow, "but, oh, the peace of that cottage after a day's work, and," laughs Mrs Bailey, "nobody could fetch you out in the middle of the night as there was no telephone!"

Mr Bailey gets up to go to the privy at the end of the garden, and while he is gone Mrs Bailey points out to me the round shaving mirror fixed just above her husband's chair, facing the window. "It took ages getting the right angle," she says. "Now he can see everything that's going on in the village!"

When Mr Bailey returns he carefully hangs up his overcoat and hat. Simultaneously I jump out of his chair, where I have been sitting.

"We were the same as children!" laughs Mrs Bailey. "I was one of seven and the moment we saw our father coming up the lane, if any of us was in his chair we'd be out of it in a flash!"

She gets up now to fill their hot-water bottle. "When I was a child," she recalls, "we used to fill the warming pan with red hot coals and slide it around between the sheets just before going to bed. You didn't let it rest because the copper pan would get very hot and scorch the sheets."

Mr Bailey hasn't worked for years. "He had bad rheumatism for he doesn't know how long," his wife explains. "But he always fought against it. It wears itself out you know. He would sometimes get on a bicycle and then not be able to get off it. Or it would take him an hour to get to the shops. Then once I whipped his back with nettles. 'Harder! Harder!' he cried. And he hasn't had rheumatism since, and you're what now, George? Ninety!"

1972

JANUARY 29ᵀᴴ

Back from London where I have been very busy teaching a theatre course to American students from Oberlin College, Ohio. I call on the Baileys and find George wheezing as he gets in buckets of coal, his blue eyes watering.

"She's not been good all week," he says of Mrs B. "I keep in the warm as much as I can. But God is good. He takes care of us."

I sit with him by the fire.

"Though you've been out of sight, you've not been out of mind. We remember you every day. The telegraph poles and cables get blown down, but there's one Cable that never breaks."

He adds that the bottle of medicine I bought them weeks ago was suddenly there when Mrs B. needed it, and they felt so grateful to me for getting it. I offer to bring in the coal for him tomorrow.

JANUARY 31ST

Albert Thomas appears, shyly lifting his pork pie hat off his head then pushing it back on again.

"Got you a rabbit. Will you skin it or shall I?"

Later he reappears, freshly shaved, pink and shining, his dark eyes glowing, bearing the skinned rabbit in an orange plastic bowl.

I cook the rabbit and take a bowlful over to the Baileys, get in their coal, empty the ashes from the grate, collect the newspaper and do some shopping for them. Mrs Bailey, with sores on her lips and looking very pale, is seated by the fire. Snow begins to fall softly in large breadcrumb flakes. It is very cold.

FEBRUARY 1ST

It sounds like rain but when I get up and look out of the window it is still snowing; a hard, dry, drifting snow. Water comes out of the tap in a thin trickle. Jean Thomas says this means a slight freeze but keep the tap running and it will thaw out. Mrs Bailey had wanted me to get her some stewing steak but because of the drifts Ruth does not risk driving in to Knighton. Instead I take the Baileys two cod steaks in cheese sauce from my fridge. I rake out their ashes, lay a new fire for them, then break some frozen Brussels sprouts from their garden for them to have with the fish.

Next day when I call on them, the fire is burning and two kettles are simmering on the trivet. Mrs Bailey has had twenty-four hours of neuralgia on top of the sickness, "but if we can just weather today I think we shall be alright". Mr Bailey thanks me and says again that never a day goes by but they remember me.

"God knows our wants. Doctors can't do everything. God knows our needs. After forty years of married life I can testify to His faithfulness. May you have a safe journey back and every blessing."

I kiss him on his bald pate and shake his hand.

MAY 17ᵀᴴ

I get up early before sunrise and go exploring on my bike. As the sun comes up over the hills the sheep grow long shadows. In the lane two ravens fly up from a half-eaten lamb that lies with its paws neatly crossed, its eyes closed, as though sleeping; but its rib cage has been ripped open and the bloody entrails scattered.

High up, as I follow the old forest track, a cuckoo flies past with its stiff wooden body and a jerky clap of its wings, its cry followed by a sound as though it is clearing its throat. On the top of a fir tree, poised like a sentinel keeping watch, a robin is singing, while further down it is answered by another. It is almost eight by the time I return. Standing there is Albert Thomas. Freshly shaven, sniffing the air, he grins and says, "I've never seen you on a bike before!"

Later in the day I hear a crying of sheep, like the roar of a crowd at a football match, and so Mother and I go up the lane towards Dolassey Farm to see if the shearing has begun. Hundreds of sheep are crowded by the old barns, crying ceaselessly, from the high pitch of the lambs to the deep baa-ing of the rams and ewes, like the wild lament of bagpipes. The endless crying of "Mère! Mère! Mère!" sounds like French children calling for their mothers.

I work all afternoon in the garden and then go to lie on the hammock, listening to the rain on the awning.

Mother comes to join me. I make a tray of tea and we sit cradled in rugs, enjoying the snugness. With my father departed she is more relaxed, but each time I visit I can see that she is lonely. Never having learned to drive, and with no buses, she is entirely dependent on others.

"When you're gone," she says, "I open all the doors and then it doesn't seem so lonely. Then later I shut them."

Yesterday, when I was working in my study on the latest *Odd and Elsewhere* book, I smelt cooking.

"I felt so hungry," my mother said, "so I cooked myself some bacon and tomatoes and fried bread. It's because I've got company."

The Sunday after Ascension

I go to Holy Communion. I can hear Brian Williams, the forester, and the Rector talking in the vestry, and when Mr and Mrs Watson arrive the Rector jokes, "Here comes the choir!" He then asks Mrs Watson if she knows a hymn. But Mrs Watson doesn't know this particular hymn. "Oh, surely you know it?" says the Rector in some surprise, and starts to sing the melody without the words. Mrs Watson then picks it up, followed by Brian Williams, and they go on la-la-ing away in the vestry.

At the end of the service Brian stops to talk with the Rector about how difficult the hymn was.

"Trouble is," says the Rector, "there are so few hymns for Ascension that one hasn't much choice."

I sigh gently and wonder if it matters. Why do we have to stumble painfully through an unfamiliar hymn, both words and tune, for the sake of being seen, as it were, wearing the right clothes?

From my study window I watch Albert clearing away the huge holly hedge. I go out to help him drag away the branches into the churchyard where they will make a bonfire. He thrusts his way in among the laurel, elder and holly, grinning as he pulls the cord on his chainsaw, getting it roaring and growling, sawdust flying. He then takes a large axe and cuts V shapes into the trunks, ready for chopping down.

In the dusk we pause to drink some cider; he smokes a cigarette. He tells me of a saying in Radnorshire that if you get thunder before Christmas it means a mild winter, "but I prefer a hard winter, as you can then get an early spring. We once had snow here for ten weeks and no traffic could get through."

Shortly after this, Jean Hughes, a Quaker friend, drives us to Devannor Farm, up in the hills, where the Methodists still hold a service once a month in the front parlour as they did in Wesley's day. The parlour is a long room with high settles and a large rectangular table in the centre on which, under white cloths, are small chalice cups and a plate of cut squares of bread. There is a Welsh dresser with shelves of blue and white china, a tall but silent grandfather clock, and portraits of John Wesley on the wall.

Mr Quiriple, the Methodist minister, stands in a black gown at a portable desk on which rests a large, old-fashioned Bible wrapped in cloth. Behind him is a window filled with geraniums, and on the sill outside a marmalade cat licking its paws. Mrs Griffiths, aged seventy-seven, the matriarch of a large family, enters last, bent double, and as she closes the door she places a long draught excluder, made from a stuffed stocking, at its base. She then takes her seat for the service, closing her eyes, opening them only when we sing a hymn, which is accompanied on a harmonium by one of her daughters.

The congregation is made up mainly of several generations of the Griffiths family. Gwyn, the smallest of the children, investigates the chimney and then disappears under the table. We are seated on a high settle in one corner alongside a highly coloured print depicting the Broad and Narrow ways: the Broad being a great highway of people dancing, at the end of which the flames of Hell are seen leaping into the sky. We sing several hymns and there is a short sermon for the children, followed by prayers, and then a longer sermon for the grown-ups and, finally, the Communion service. The plate of bread squares is taken first to Mrs Griffiths, and so on, according to seniority. It is like a simple family meal and in the silence we can hear a robin singing. Afterwards we all have tea, seated around the table, discussing Temperance, control of the young, and other appropriate matters.

Driving back, I recall how recently at the Friends Meeting House in Hampstead I was moved to speak about the gentility of Quakers. Don't we all, I said, tend to fashion our own form of Christianity, to see what we want to see, and to ignore those sayings of Jesus, or those facts of history, that do not fit into our expectations? Hence, in part, of course, the many schisms, or branches, of Christianity.

But the more we can learn and discover, and the more we are able to consider the experience and traditions of others, the more we can appreciate unity in diversity.

Albert has ploughed, and harrowed the back garden, swinging the tractor round in sweeps. He will now plant it with a crop of mustard seed, plough it all in, and next spring, after raking, plant it with grass seed.

JULY 28TH

I arrive back from adjudicating the National Drama Festival of Zambia and spend five hours mowing and weeding. In Llandrindod I observe a short man in striped trousers, a black coat with many badges pinned to the lapels, and a red silk handkerchief flopping out of his top pocket, talking in a loud voice to everyone as he processes down the street, as though he were a very important dignitary, greeting people, crossing the street to wave to a car and then saluting. I discover that he was once the postman.

On Saturday I finish painting the double gates at the back. Mr Powell, walking down the lane, stops, his pale eyes gleaming.

"Black? Black paint? Why are you using black paint? Those gates were always green."

"Well they're black now, Mr Powell!"

He asks how my Mother is and I reply that she is very lonely.

"How old is your mother?"

"I don't know," I reply. I do know but she'd be mad at me if I let on to anyone.

"She must be getting on?" he counters.

"We all are, Mr Powell. We all are."

Later in the afternoon I go up to see Mr Duggan at Pentreland, and Mrs Duggan tells me that Mr Powell is very inquisitive.

"He comes up here and noses around. Once he asked, 'How many sheep have you got?' And I replied, 'You'd better count them!' and on another occasion he asked, 'How much did you pay for them?'"

Alfred Duggan is bedridden as the result of an accident. He lies in a double bed, flat on his back, and can't even turn on his side. There is a machine that operates a ripple mattress to prevent bedsores. I ask him whether he ever gets restless and he laughs, "I can't even move!" He seems so patient and cheerful, lying there helpless, month after month. He has a switch for the television but he never has the ripple bed on at night once his wife Ann joins him, in case they fall asleep and something goes wrong. He has a mirror above the fireplace so he can see what is happening in the lane. He used to have another upstairs so he could see everything in the valley. "I could see you working in your garden!" he laughs. They have about twenty-five acres and his wife, helped by their son who comes up regularly, looks after the sheep, the house and everything.

AUGUST 9TH

The day of the Pen-y-Bont races at Crossgates. The rain pelts down and there is a hiss of tyres on mud, while the field used for parking is so churned up that cars slither and get stuck and have to be hauled out.

There is a primitive racecourse around the field and on a bank is what is euphemistically called the Grandstand: a crude wooden structure with a rusting corrugated iron roof. On this are assembled about two hundred people, looking like a Cruikshank drawing. On the other side is a platform with a railing where the judges stand, wearing long trench coats, trilby hats and bootlace ties.

The Master of Ceremonies is very Welsh, and full of wisecracks.

"Please take your horses into the paddock! Sorry about the hold-up, everybody! Now, Jockeys, hurry up and get weighed. The bookies have to be back in business for the next race!"

Continuing to declaim through a microphone he begins to describe the various horses.

"*Ease-Away*, the property of Mr Higgins of Ross-on-Wye: we have had the pleasure of this horse winning at Abergavenny two weeks ago. Ladies and Gentlemen, if you would like, you can see this and other horses as the stewards bring them into the paddock. *Our Pick*, the fastest horse, will now go into the finals, the only lady rider this afternoon."

The judges return and the MC comments, "These honourable men, the judges, are now returned to their posts. I hope they have had nothing stronger than tea!" – at which point one of the judges slips and everyone laughs.

We watch a Trotting match, the riders leaning well back on their curious chariots splashed with mud. The rain drenches down, children cry, while mothers clutch the smallest children in their arms to keep them out of the mud. The MC goes on chatting. "Local tradesmen used to have trotting matches on a Sunday morning," he tells us. "That's how they started. Now, here's a very nice little bay mare, looking very well …" – but not its jockey, a boy of eleven, who is in fact looking very white and downcast as the horse slithers from side to side as it is led to the post.

When the rain ceases, we eventually drift away to visit a sale at one of the cottages by the blacksmith's forge down by the edge of the river. All the furniture is ranged in a large circle on a bank: wooden carvers, pine and oak tables, iron bedsteads, wooden bedsteads, corner cupboards, hallstands, pictures, boxes of books; as well as a collection of china, rolling pins, and tools, laid out on a kitchen table, all sopping wet from the rain. People shelter inside the cottage where bed-linen, blankets, and a quilt made from scraps of old clothes, are for sale. Upstairs, in a back bedroom, I find a wooden shutter let into a wall. Opening it, I see straw and realise it has been used as a hen coop. Farmers gather in groups to chat, while the women sit on any available chairs. Inside the smithy, where ashes glow and spark, another small group of men stand gossiping. Laid out on planks of wood, all jumbled up, are the letters of the alphabet, line upon line, burned into the wood by red hot irons.

I walk back four miles in the drizzling rain, as car after car, most of them empty save for the driver, whizzes past without stopping.

AUGUST 15TH

There are bees coming down the kitchen chimney. Mr Thomas who has been to fit it against jackdaws, says there is honey in the chimney which means that the bees have been there some time. I telephone Powys County Council in Llandrindod Wells and they say I must ring the Town Hall. I ring the Town Hall and am passed to the Surveyor's Department but when they learn that I am at Bleddfa they say that they are the urban council and Bleddfa is outside their jurisdiction. I then ring the Rural District Council in Knighton and get the wife of a Councillor who says I must employ a beekeeper. I try the Town Hall again and they say the surveyor will ring back. When he does he also says I must either find a beekeeper or else get on to the Ministry of Agriculture and speak to their bee expert. I try the recommended beekeeper at Llanbister Road but he replies, "I have no head for heights. Try Mr Davies, the Ministry's man at Pant-yr-dwr". I say that I have already tried him at his office in Llandrindod Wells but there was no answer. "Ah, well, at this time of year he is out a lot, but ring his home."

I do this on the number given and a woman answers. "Who is this?" she asks.

I reply that my name will mean nothing to her.

"What is your name?" she persists.

"I am Mr Roose-Evans, and my mother at the Old Rectory, Bleddfa, has bees coming down her chimney."

She replies that her husband cannot climb heights as he is not insured by the Council, but to ring back later as he might be able to arrange something privately. "Ring after seven in the evening," she says.

After seven I ask the operator to get me Pant-yr-dwr 557.

A man's voice answers.

"Is that Mr Davies?"

"Oh, just a minute."

There is a pause and then a woman's voice says, "Hello?"

"Is that Mrs Davies?"

"Yes?"

"I'm Mr Roose-Evans. I rang earlier about my mother's chimney."

"I'm very sorry about your mother …"

"Might I speak to Mr Davies?"

"No!"

"But you said to ring after 7 o'clock!"

"I'm afraid you can't."

"Do you mean he won't be in tonight?"

There is a pause and then the woman says, "You can't speak to him because he's dead."

"Is that Pant-yr-dwr 557?"

"No, this is Pant-yr-dwr 559."

It is only then I realise I have rung the wrong number!

I now ring Pant-yr-dwr 557 and a woman answers.

I explain that I am Mr Roose-Evans and my mother, at the Old Rectory, Bleddfa, has bees coming down the chimney.

"Oh, you'll have to you speak to my husband."

A man comes to the phone and asks, "Who is that?"

Once again I repeat: "I am Mr Roose-Evans and my mother, who lives at the Old Rectory, Bleddfa, has bees coming down the chimney."

"Oh, dear, that's a very messy job. Newly decorated, you say the room is? Oh dear!"

He explains that he can smoke out the bees, but if the comb remains the bees will return next year.

"You will need to insert a brush to dislodge the comb and then soot, mortar, rubbish and honey will be all over the place! But I'll try and look in tomorrow morning."

AUGUST 20TH

Going to bed this evening, my mother says, "There was a big moth flew upstairs when I put out the light."

I go upstairs. "It's probably gone up into the attic."

I switch on the lights and see a large bat. I start involuntarily and come down. Mother has observed my reaction but says nothing. She knows it is a bat but still pretends it is a large moth.

"Best leave it there," she says. Last week she found a baby bat in her chamber-pot and poured boiling water on it.

I go into my study and the bat flies in. I open the French windows hoping it will fly out, but instead it flies straight at me. I wave my arms, directing it towards the window until finally it flies out. Tomorrow I will arrange to have muslin screens made for all the windows so that they can be open on hot summer evenings but bats will be prevented from flying in.

AUGUST 23RD

Finally at dusk Mr Davies, the bee man, arrives with his wife Agnes. He has a bald pate with a rim of hair like a monk's tonsure. He is wearing brown overalls, while she wears mauve trousers with a plum coloured sweater and a mauve scarf around her head. Where he is paunchy and has a tanned complexion, she has a thin pale face and sad dark eyes. While he sets to work, Agnes explains to me that her husband is an authority on bees: he gives classes, and they run a small business selling honey wholesale. They bought the village school at St Harmon as his laboratory and workshop and then built their house alongside it.

We remove the screen from the kitchen range and he places in the fireplace a chemical, like a yellow candle, in a tin full of shavings, then lights it. The chimney fills with smoke and kills the bees at once. Soot and dead bees cascade down the chimney. He now burns some papers. Suddenly there are crackles followed by small explosions, and lumps of honeycomb, soot, boiling wax and dead bees come tumbling down. The kitchen floor is caked with dead bees and soot like currants out of a burned cake. Agnes keeps picking up the bees and flinging them out of the window.

Bob Davies says, "We always have to do these jobs. No builder will touch a job like this. They won't start until we've tackled it."

He keeps repeating, "I'm very pleased with the job!"

When we put the screen back in front of the fireplace he advises boring holes in it as without ventilation the chimney shaft becomes warm and therefore makes an ideal place for a swarm.

He charges me £3.

I say to him, "I think I ought to learn how to keep bees." And so I begin attending his classes and eventually acquire three hives.

SEPTEMBER 1ST

The Rector calls to tell me that Bleddfa church has been placed on a provisional list for closure. What can be done?

Having founded the Hampstead Theatre Club on a shoestring, do I really want to get involved in trying to save a church in so isolated a situation? I promise him I will give the matter careful thought.

OCTOBER 21ST

To Chester to audition 150 people for the Mystery Plays, which are to form part of next year's Festival. I plan to reduce the cast to thirty adults plus a handful of urchin-like small boys as angels arriving on bicycles, shouting "Gloria in Excelsis Deo!" I have in mind a strong ensemble that will explode onto the stage. The last thing I want is a reverential pious approach. My aim is to bring the stories vibrantly alive.

OCTOBER 23RD

I get a train from Chester to Shrewsbury and then, with my suitcase, walk a mile out of the town, hoping to catch a lift. Rain descends torrentially. Unexpectedly a car stops and a man with bloodshot eyes offers me a lift. He has driven straight from work in Liverpool and is on his way to Michaelchurch (halfway between Hay and Hereford) to visit his first wife's grave and put flowers on it.

"I only decided on the spur of the moment. But there'll be a row with my second wife. She's Irish. She won't understand about my wanting to visit the grave. If ever you are in Liverpool, come and have a drink, but don't say where we met. She wants to know everything."

He joined the army when he was nineteen, having lied about his age, and three years later war broke out. He now works on the cranes, the same work as dockers, but he is with a different union and so doesn't get the pay of the dockers, many of whom get as much as £100 a week.

We talk quietly, with easy silences, as the rain dribbles, slides and beats against the windscreen. He had intended to drop me off at Leominster but in the end decides to drive me all the way home to Bleddfa, and then retrace his route.

OCTOBER 27TH

I awake to the sound of rain. Collecting our milk from the Post Office, Jean Thomas says everyone predicts a hard winter, while the experts say we are returning to the ice age! More power cuts are anticipated. During the cuts last winter, Jean and Ruth took up oil painting, having bought a kit from the stationer's in Knighton. "It would come one or two in the morning and we'd totally lost ourselves! It's very relaxing. I paint scenes from memory. I couldn't do still life, like that bottle of pickles there!"

OCTOBER 30ᵀᴴ

I visit Alfred Duggan, who is as cheerful as ever. He tells me he likes cold potatoes left over from lunch fried up for his supper. He used to have a very sweet tooth but now likes ordinary sponge cakes and plain bread-and-butter for his tea. I offer to bring him a bottle of perry tomorrow.

NOVEMBER 13ᵀᴴ

Hywel and I go walking at dusk along the lane as far as Albert's brother's farm. High on the skyline are the outlines of sheep. The sky on the horizon is a wash of yellow brushed with charcoal streaks. We meet Albert, out hedging, late.

"Have you got a match?" he asks, pipe in mouth. He is a complete silhouette. Little Pip, his dog who follows him everywhere, comes scurrying along the lane, a bundle of blackness, like part of the advancing night.

1973

MARCH 1ST

Mother comes into my study at the Old Rectory, holding a photograph of me aged seven, when I had a mass of auburn curls: it is me as she would have liked me to remain. She stands behind me, putting her hand through my hair, saying, "Your hair's still silky," and then, out of her pain, cries, "I wish I could do something!" She feels so outside everything in my life, even though I share all my friends with her. What she laments is the lost paradise, the time when I was small and wholly dependent on her, when we were so close, mother and child, a world within a world.

On each visit from London I travel with the burden of my mother's pain and do not know the answer. The Old Rectory is too lonely for her, the situation too isolated, since she cannot drive and there is no bus, so she is dependent on others for lifts. Deep down, I realise she wants to be in her own home and not in mine, yet I have already found her two homes and she got bored and restless with both. Would she be happier if she had her own bungalow?

MARCH 3ᴿᴰ

After long discussions, Hywel and I suggest to the Rector that if he really wants to save the church there is no good waiting until it is declared redundant: by then it will be too late. We suggest that the building, while continuing to be used for worship, should be developed as a Centre for Sacred Art, with exhibitions, study days, retreats, and other special events. I realise that if I don't do something, nobody else will. Surprisingly, the Rector supports this and suggests I get in touch with George Pace, who is the one of the leading church architects in the country and who fairly recently carried out the re-ordering of New Radnor church. When he leaves, I sit down and write a letter …

MARCH 15ᵀᴴ

The Rector invites me to be Correspondent (secretary) to the village school, which belongs to the Church in Wales, and I begin to pass on the children's books I'm sent to review for the *Financial Times*. One day I am invited by Norma Beedon, the teacher, to lunch with the children. Arriving a little too early while she is still teaching, I say softly to the children, "I am not here." I sit on one of the low chairs and look at the model of an Indian encampment that the children have been making, with an upside down shuttlecock as a wigwam. On one wall is a round clock and underneath a sign, which proclaims:

HERE IS THE CLOCK
IT IS THE SCHOOL CLOCK
THE CLOCK TELLS THE TIME

Along the windowsill are jam jars with twigs standing in water, and hand-printed notices against each: Oak, Ash, Sycamore, Elder and so on. More curiously, there is a handmade sign, obviously something made more than fifty years ago:

THREE THINGS FROM OLD PERSIA
(three things the ancient Persians taught their children from the age of five)
1. To manage a horse well
2. To shoot dexterously with a bow
3. To speak the truth

A high fender surrounds the iron stove, its central pipe disappearing above into the wall. There is a small, square door for access to the flue.

One of the boys, Adam, starts talking to me, and little Robert Gittoes from the Mill says to him, "Why are you talking to yourself?"

"I'm not!" replies Adam. "I'm talking to James!"

"But he isn't here! He said so himself!" says Robert with a grin.

Mrs Morris arrives with the school lunches. They are now forty-five pence a time and only seven of the children have them; the rest bring plastic boxes containing sandwiches (egg, tomatoes, jam, cake, Kit Kat, and apples). I sit with Colin, Christopher and Robert and we have chicken, and then some sloppy pudding.

I retire upstairs to discuss school matters with Mrs Beedon in the cottage where the Baileys used to live (they have now moved to a Council bungalow at Crossgates.)

There is a knock at the door. It is Kim.

"Please, Mrs Beedon, I've got a sore throat."

"I'm very sorry, Kim. There's nothing I can do except give you sympathy and suggest you gargle with salt water."

"Where will I get the salt?"

"Ask Mrs Morris downstairs."

Kim goes, and shortly afterwards there is another tap on the door. It is five-year-old Tom, who has crawled up the stairs on his stomach.

"May I play with the sand bowl?" he asks.

Given permission, he crawls backwards, grinning.

Another knock and Kim reappears with a glass of water.

"I've put pepper and salt in it," she says.

"Oh well," sighs Mrs Beedon, "I don't expect the pepper will hurt. Off you go!"

When she has gone, Mrs Beedon turns to me. "Poor Kim! She's always worrying about something. It's a crisis of identity, I think. She and Adam both have different fathers and she sometimes says, 'We've got three Daddies.'"

The next day, two of the children call on me with a note from Mrs Beedon: Janet Lewis of the Village Farm, who suffers from depressions, is going into hospital tomorrow for a brain scan. It will only take an hour but she is frightened. So I invite Janet in for a cup of coffee and a chat and then walk her back to the cottage where she stands looking lost.

I realise some physical gesture of reassurance is needed so I put my arms around her and give her a kiss. Richard, her husband, who is backing a trailer full of manure out of the barn with his tractor, turns and waves.

MARCH 20TH

I attend a Parish Meeting in the village school, where we all sit on low seats. The chairman, Mr Hergest, the black-smith who stammers, announces that a new chairman ought to be elected to replace him, as this is the final year of the Bleddfa Parish Meeting. Next year, 1974, it has to merge with the Parish Council of Llangunllo, our neighbouring village. Mr Gittoes from the Mill, wearing a raincoat over his suit and a cap on his head, says to Mr Hergest, "I reckon you'd better stand again!" So Mr Hergest grins and crosses from left to right of the room to sit in the Chairman's place, next to the Secretary.

The main business is then carried out, including the tenders for the Parish Field at Fishponds. Folded slips of paper and notes sealed in envelopes are opened, and the name and address of each applicant read out, followed by the sum of money each is prepared to pay by way of rent. In the end Mr Bufton gets the field for £50.

It is now time to discuss the annual Sports Event and at once everybody starts talking. I stand up and ask the chairman when it is to be.

"The races take place at 3 pm on July 21st, which is the end of the school term," he replies, "but the main problem is what to do with the older children, those of fifteen and sixteen."

It transpires that there are some forty children in the area. Free tea is provided for local pensioners, "though only six turned up last year," grumbles Mr Gittoes. "And we had to cancel the egg-and-spoon race," chuckles Mr Hergest, "because the children ate the eggs!"

It turns out that the real problem is that the menfolk are likely to be harvesting. Albert Thomas, speaking with a strong voice, argues that it means a lot of work for just the few people left preparing the food, "and then folks who never do a darn thing come along, just because they can get something for nothing!"

As Chairman, Mr Hergest brings it all to a halt by declaring, "I suppose we'd better just carry on as we always have done. After all, the children seem to enjoy it."

"Perhaps August would be a better month?" suggests another farmer.

"Ah, but then the kiddies would be off on their summer holidays."

The school clock ticks away as everyone ruminates. Prizes and presents for a draw are then discussed. I offer to help here with some of my books for the children.

"It's a busy time just now," comments another. "What with lambing, folks are bit tired. I reckon we ought to hold another meeting later on about the Sports."

And with this the Parish Meeting is readily adjourned and everyone hurries over to the Hundred House for a pint.

Inside one of the byres on Farmer George's farm, Albert Thomas and his father are shaving fleece from under the back legs of ewes and clipping their hooves against foot rot. Each ewe is grabbed by the front legs, turned upside down, and shaved with a pair of electric clippers. Mr Thomas then takes the ewe from Albert and, holding it between his legs, cuts roughly into the black hooves with clippers, sometimes cutting too deeply so there is blood.

"It is good for them to bleed," he tells me. "The hooves sometimes grow so long that they double back on themselves."

Finally the ewes are released back into the fields and there is a great commotion as they try to find their lambs. Albert and his father take a break for a cigarette, gazing at the valley and all their sheep, and quietly talking. "See those two black lambs there?" says Albert. "Them's Beth's and Leah's."

APRIL 22ND

Albert arrives to plough the back garden. He brings two tyres and makes a bonfire of the apple branches. At first there is a tall pillar of smoke; then suddenly it explodes into whirling, orange-coloured flames, with sparks shooting outwards. With his trilby hat firmly wedged on his head, Albert lifts large branches and stacks the pile higher, carrying on even when it starts to rain. And then the rain is followed by an unexpected shower of hailstones, like homeopathic pillules. Beth and Leah, his two small daughters, come to watch from a careful distance. Leah, aged two, stands with the thumb of one hand in her mouth and the other hand in her pocket, while Beth puts a protective arm around her little sister's shoulders.

Hywel, who has been busy planting shrubs and clearing the area by the door, invites Albert into the kitchen for a cup of tea, and we learn from him how local farmers have been cheating on agricultural grants. If something was eligible for a seventy-five per cent grant then they would up their expenses so that they could qualify for a hundred per cent grant.

He tells of two brothers, both farmers, with adjoining farms, who regularly cheated with their cows in the days when there used to be a grant per head of cattle. Once a year an official would go round the farms to check. He'd count, say, forty head of cattle on the one brother's farm, and then drive around the hillside to the other brother's farm to count the cattle there. In the meantime, while he was on his way round, the first brother would drive *his* forty cattle over the hill and down into his brother's farm. In this way they used to get grants for eighty head of cattle even though they only had forty between them. Eventually, however, they were found out.

MAY 4ᵀᴴ

I have been telephoning the Old Rectory from London. I ring at intervals throughout the day but no answer. So I call Ruth Casson at the Post Office and she goes up to see what's the matter. She rings back to say that my mother is her usual self but has gone stone deaf. What does this bode I wonder?

MAY 5ᵀᴴ

On arrival from London I find my mother gay and full of humour about what has proved to be only temporary deafness. She had stuffed cotton wool into her ears and then tried to remove it with tweezers. Dr Davies says her ears were packed with wax and inflamed. He has removed the cotton wool and says he will syringe out the wax once the inflammation has gone down.

Next morning we breakfast together and she giggles every time I have to put my mouth to her ear. With what resilience she takes this set-back. She prepares a special tea, helps me in the garden, and holds back her tears at the thought of my returning to London.

AUGUST 11ᵀᴴ

Back at the Old Rectory I hear Mother seated at the piano singing the hymn "Art thou weary, art thou languid?" Suddenly she stops, lowers her hands to her side, and begins talking to herself, "Such bitterness … the sins of the father." She begins to play other hymns, singing out key phrases such as "Comfort ye … rest for the weary". Suddenly I realise something is wrong. It is almost as though she has been drinking. I run upstairs and see an empty bottle of mandrax sleeping pills by her bedside. I ring Dr Davies who says, "Get her to drink mustard and salt in water and I'll be right round."

She drinks a lot of the mixture without protest, seeming half-asleep. When Dr Davies arrives we carry her into the kitchen. "Oh, you are a heavy girl!" he jests, and props her on a stool by the sink. Removing her dentures, he rinses them and puts them on one side, then fills a glass vessel with water. He inserts one end of a red tube into the water and the other into her mouth. I try to hold her hands as she fights back with such strength. However, the water does the trick and she vomits. It looks as though she has only taken one, or at the most two, of the sleeping tablets. She gets up, like an automaton, and walks jerkily away; I support her from behind. Finally we get her seated in a chair, back in her sitting-room. We check all her medications and then Dr Davies spends an hour sitting with her, joking, getting her to laugh, to relax and talk.

"It's the loneliness," she says. "I get so depressed."

One moment she is smiling winningly at him out of those cornflower-blue eyes and then, the next, her face crumples, tears well up, and she shakes violently from within.

"He has a tongue that can slay," she says of me. "No one knows. They think him so charming. Calls himself a Christian."

"You should hit him back!" jokes the doctor.

"His words hurt!"

"But you must remember that words are his profession."

"I'm sensitive. Always have been. You can't help your nature. I want a little cottage with my own front door and curtains and to be able to pay my own rates and bills and be mistress in my own home – not caretaker of someone else's. Since Mr and Mrs Bailey have moved to

Crossgates it has been so lonely. I only took two tablets, to forget. I would never take more."

Gradually, patiently, he gets her to relax and laugh. Later she eats a hearty meal that I cook for her, gives me a great hug, and goes to bed.

I marvel at Dr Davies' devotion to his patients. It is not surprising that stories of his kindness are legion: turning out at all hours of the day or night, and taking time to listen to people. As a GP he is almost the last of his kind, the last of a generation of family doctors. He and his wife Alison first met at Oxford where he was a junior doctor and she was a sister on the paediatric ward at the Radcliffe Infirmary. After the birth of their only son she suffered intermittently for the rest of her life from post-natal depression, and at intervals had to be admitted to the mental hospital at Talgarth. He would drive over the hills to visit her and, on the way back, dispirited by these occasions, would stop off at the little church at Rhulen, up in the hills between Hay and Painscastle and just sit there. Although agnostic, he tells me that he has always found great peace there, in what Philip Larkin in his poem *Church Going* describes as "a serious house on serious earth".

AUGUST 13TH

Farmer George calls to see me. It's in response to a polite note about the bird-scaring device he has fitted on the hill opposite, which goes off all night, every night, even when no birds are flying. I've asked him if it could be switched off at night, now that the crops are ripe. It was set up earlier in the year when oats were sown in order to prevent hundreds of rooks eating the grain.

"I've switched it off now!" he says with a sad smile as we sit in the kitchen over a cup of tea. "We don't live a long time and none of us wants to cause offence."

He inspects the new lawn at the front where once, when there was a Rector living here, there had been a U-shaped drive for the carriages. He remembers the house and garden well from when John Williams was alive, for his wife's aunt was John Williams' sister.

"Old Mr Williams had two sons but both died young. One was mental and the other was mongol – he couldn't walk so he had to go about in a wheelchair. He used to sit at the bottom of the garden gate there – this was before all the trees grew up – where there used to be a stile, and watch the goings-on in the village. He died in 1932. He was only seventeen. It really cut up the old man when the two boys died, much more than when his wife of fifty years died. You cry less when you get to our age. Oh, yes, I used to call on him every day.

"I also remember that hut at the bottom of the garden. Very useful for courting! I did quite a bit in there!"

He asks me how the apple trees are bearing in the back garden. "I remember as boys we often took quite a few from the top two trees."

He has always lived here, and his parents before him, on the same farm. "My parents were devoted to each other and I can never recall hearing a cross word. Wherever my father went he always brought back a present for my mother. It might only be a bar of chocolate in those days, but there was always something. And I have kept up the practice. I always bring back something to Joyce, my wife.

"I never wanted to be a farmer. If I could have my life over I wouldn't be a farmer, but that's all there was at the time."

"What would you like to have done?"

"Surgery. A vet or something of that. There's a great satisfaction in being able to save an animal. Caring for it, injecting it, seeing it recover."

He tells me that Albert, whom he employs, enjoys working for me at the Old Rectory, "and it helps him earn some extra money. Farm wages aren't very high. We can't afford to pay more."

The next morning Hywel and I get up at six thirty and go past Neuadd, down to the stream, and then climb up above Higher Storling. As the sun rises at the end of the valley we see trees and bushes emerging out of the mist. The grass is wet with dew, and the stillness of the early morning is heightened by the bleating of sheep. Hywel stands, hand on hip, surveying the valley. Then, back at the Old Rectory, we cook a breakfast of bacon, eggs and fried bread, with toast, marmalade and coffee, and it is all ready by the time Mother comes down.

In the evening we dine with Jack Hollins. One of eleven children – the eleventh was christened Undecimus – the family lived in Nottingham. For many years he was a musical accompanist, until he retired to live at Beguildy, near Knighton, in what was grandly called The Town House: a converted stable, where he taught himself to cook and subsequently ran a small restaurant. He tells how, when he first set up his new business, official forms would keep arriving asking questions such as, "How much parking space do you have?" "How will your provisions be delivered?" and so on. He scribbled his answer to the last question on the form: "Thrown off the local bus once a week!" When he received an income tax form, the first and only one in his life, he worked out some sums and received a letter back asking, "How did you arrive at these figures?" to which he answered "By the process of arithmetic!" He never heard another word.

The stable is divided into three bays: the first is where guests have drinks; the second has a round gaming table where one sits to eat; and the third, hidden by carpets and tapestries, is where he does the washing-up. Along the other side are the kitchen ranges; and hanging from the beams are canisters labelled Dry Beans, Herbs, Pasta, Dried Mushrooms, Grated Almonds, Sugar, and alongside them polythene bags labelled Birdseed, Peanuts, etc.

Wearing a striped blue and white apron darkened with grease (does it ever get washed? I wonder) spread over his curving stomach, with a grimy oven cloth over one shoulder, he converses with his guests as he cooks. He runs the restaurant less as a business venture and more as a hobby. Indeed, he is very choosy about who he allows to eat here. On one famous occasion a group was so loud and raucous that at the end of the meal, when asked for the bill, he scribbled "Two shillings and sixpence. And I hope never to see you again!"

Frequently, because I still cannot drive, Jack insists on

coming over to Bleddfa to collect my mother, Hywel and myself, taking us back for dinner and then returning us home afterwards. Travelling with him can be hazardous, however. On one occasion, seeing another car approaching along a narrow lane, he simply mounted the bank!

There was a time before he acquired the stable when he rented a cottage from the neighbouring farmer. Each week he would buy a copy of the *Farmers Weekly*, rumple it a bit, and then take it to them, saying they might like to have it. "They were so mean they never even took a paper. Sometimes I would drop in on them and find the whole family seated in a semi-circle round the fire. The parents would be sitting in wooden carvers on either side of the fireplace, while the nine children – two sisters and seven brothers, their ages varying from twelve to thirty – would each be reading a single page of the *Farmers Weekly*. They would tear out one page after another and pass it on, regardless of the continuity of the articles – and there they would all sit, each with a torn out page!"

He tells us about the black man he once saw as a child in the marketplace at Nottingham, whose name was Quacko, and whose advertising sign read: "Teeth extracted painlessly with thumb and forefinger only." "He had such huge hands," Jack says. "It was difficult to imagine how he could even get them into anyone's mouth!"

He relates how all through the 1930s he used to go once a week to conduct a choir of miners in the village hall on Ruardean Hill. He loved watching the miners on their way to work: "You'd see them coming down hills and through the Forest of Dean, their lanterns flickering in the dark."

Once, trudging in deep snow the four miles back to Cinderford, he had just got as far as the Speech House and was walking between two lines of trees when, in the dark, he heard a whistle to his left which was then repeated to his right. He walked forward in the dark through the snow, along the avenue of trees, and as he went the whistles preceded him the whole way, first on the left, and then on the right. He saw no one and never discovered who, what or why. But, as he adds, "the wood was full of haunts".

SEPTEMBER 19TH

The Rector has called a special meeting of the Parochial Church Council to put the George Pace scheme for re-ordering the church to the vote. If agreed, it can then go forward to the Diocesan authority in Brecon for formal permission – what I believe is technically known as a Faculty.

Torch in hand, I make my way to the church from the Old Rectory. Being the first to arrive I switch on the lights and the single heater. The Rector arrives soon after wearing a cassock and cape, followed by Brian Williams. We sit in the front pew and watch a bat. Suddenly it folds up like an umbrella being closed and disappears into a small crack in a beam. Brian says he lets them fly in and out of his bedroom window: "After all, if they can come in then they can find their way out. But the wife doesn't like it." The Rector tells us he sleeps with a sheet over his head, pulled round his face, leaving just a hole for breathing.

Finally Mr and Mrs Watson arrive: "We nearly didn't come, Rector!"

After a short prayer, the minutes of the last meeting – a year ago – are read and various items of business are discussed. Then the matter turns to my suggestion that if the building is not to be declared redundant it has to be used in other ways, which is why I have proposed that it be developed as a Centre for Sacred Art.

"I dunno," says Mrs Watson. "Oughtn't the rest of the parish to be here? There's so few of us."

"They had their chance," replies the Rector. "If they had been at church on Sunday they'd have heard the announcement."

"Got to move with the times, Mother," says Mr Watson.

"Oh well…" replies his wife dubiously. "If it brings in the young people."

Motion carried!

Next day the coalman calls, a cheerful, curly-headed, blue-eyed man in his twenties, who says, "I've got a terrible cold. I would have thought I'd have sweated it off by now. Still, I'll try and wash it away tonight."

He is up at seven every morning and doesn't finish till seven in the evening. "It takes me an hour and a half to get clean. I'm a qualified mechanic, passed all my exams, but it's terrible being in the garage all day long. I like having the lorry and being out and about in the open. I'm busy all year round. Coal is cheaper in the summer – so, up to the first of October, that's the busiest time. I also deliver hurdles."

NOVEMBER 16ᵀᴴ

The day of my driving test in Llandrindod Wells. I pass! Mother bursts into tears. Hywel is amazed.

NOVEMBER 20ᵀᴴ

The Diocese of Swansea and Brecon has granted a Faculty and so I issue a statement to the press, entitled *A First Stage*:

What follows is the first stage in the renewed life of one small Welsh village church, St Mary Magdalene's in Bleddfa, Radnorshire.

The earliest record of the church here is 1281, and of the present building the nave dates from the early part of the thirteenth century. The church receives mention in the Shell Guidebook to Wales, and it was at this end of the valley in 1402 that Owain Glyndwr led his soldiers to fight against the Earl of Mortimer and his English troops.

Our plans for Bleddfa church aim not only at creating a more intimate space for worship but also a flexible area that can be used for the performances of choral music, chamber concerts, exhibitions of art and crafts. It is also part of our plan to use the building as a centre for meditation and prayer. The village inn, the Hundred House, provides an excellent restaurant, while accommodation is available at the inn and at neighbouring farms and cottages.

If our plans are carried through successfully we hope that others will be encouraged to follow our example, not merely to preserve an ancient building but to explore the creative potential of our Welsh churches and chapels for a variety of purposes. In England, churches are being declared redundant at the rate of two a week, or over a hundred each year. In Radnorshire there are many churches like Bleddfa that are threatened with being declared redundant, closed, and eventually razed to the ground. We believe that it is our task to try and preserve some of these buildings for those who come after us.

DECEMBER 7TH

Mr Griffin, the chimney sweep from Knighton, comes to clean the two sitting-room chimneys for £1.75. He carries in an electric hoover, a big black iron contraption like a Calor gas cylinder, together with a collection of blackened but still yellowish rods which screw one into the other. It takes eleven of them to reach the top of our chimneys.

First he lays a narrow sheet of polythene on which to walk from the door to the fireplace, and then in front of the hearth he puts down a large square cloth. He next loosens the soot at the top of the fireplace with a brush so that it falls into the grate. Taking a grimy cloth he fixes this around the fireplace with sellotape. In the centre of this cloth is a sleeve through which he passes the first of the canes, vigorously pushing it up the chimney, rotating it to the right.

"You may have to do this yourself one day," he says. "You never know! So always rotate it to the right; if you twiddle to your left it will come unscrewed."

Now he adds another cane and pushes higher, rotating again to the right. Then the next cane, and so on, one after the other. Bits of stone, mortar and plaster come tumbling down. Apparently in the old days they used to line the inside of the chimney with plaster which made the flues easier to clean since the soot didn't stick in the crevices.

"When you feel the brush go free, then you know it's at the top. If the flue twists and turns a lot it may be difficult to judge. In which case you need to go outside and look up to see if it has emerged from the chimney-top. Sometimes, especially with ornamental chimneys, the wire gets stuck – there, you see! So you push it up, twist a little to the right and then down. There!"

Cane by cane is now removed until finally the brush is down. He removes the cloth and behind it is a mound of soot and plaster. "Good old-fashioned builders would use a mixture of cow-dung with the plaster so that it stretches with the heat," he comments.

I ask him why the back of the fireplace has cracked.

"Ah! Let me tell you a secret. When you are installing a grate you need to place at the back a sheet of corrugated paper. This will burn away but it will leave just enough space for the fireback to expand under the heat. Builders who don't know this secret just shove the metal up against the wall and so the fireback cracks as it expands."

He tells me how he used to be a pig-killer, but when the law came in about humane killing of pigs it meant buying a gun to shoot into the pig's brain. "I reckon this humane way of killing pigs is less good, as the pig doesn't bleed properly. Under the old method when the pig's throat was cut and the pig struggled, so the blood would pour out. Under this new method a lot of blood remains in the veins. That was when I decided to build up my chimney sweeping practice and invest in this hoover."

DECEMBER 14TH

Alfred Duggan has died. I go up the hill to Pentreland to call on Ann. She is there with her son Vernon, and Alfred's brother and sister-in-law. Like everyone else, I step from mat to mat so as not to dirty the pale blue linoleum. I go with Ann into the front room, which I have visited so often. The curtains are drawn and there on the floor, at the side of their double bed, Alfred lies in a narrow coffin, wearing a white silk robe edged with purple, which also frames his head, so that he looks like a priest vested for Mass.

His arms are stretched forward, the hands clenched. He is an ivory colour, his mouth fallen in because his dentures have been removed. He looks severe, ascetic, and yet also like a baby in its cradle, the coffin being lined with white silk. I kneel by the side while Ann remains standing, her eyes closed. When I get up I hold her hand for a moment, and she says, "He died so peacefully. He didn't have any pain for two days previously and he said something about having a vision."

The lid of the coffin lies on the bed and engraved on the plaque is his age: *61 years.*

"So young!" I murmur.

Ann says how sad it was that he should have missed out so many years of their life together when he could have enjoyed things.

We go back into the sitting room where there is an old-fashioned range with a small oven, all gleaming and polished, as is everything in this house. In one corner of the room are hooks in the beams from which hams used to hang. "Alfred used to say that those hooks with hams on them made the best pictures!"

They don't know how many will turn up for the funeral tomorrow and the tea afterwards. Alfred's coffin will be taken to Zion Chapel this evening and lie there overnight.

NEXT DAY:

There is a land fairer than day,
In the sweet by and bye,
We shall meet on that beautiful shore

From inside the crowded chapel we hear the words of this familiar hymn. The wind blows icily and those of us gathered outside shiver, or stamp our feet to keep warm. One small group of men talk throughout the service, all through the address and prayers, as they survey the line of cars in the road below and comment on smoke rising from the chimneys of Upper and Middle Storling at the opposite side of the valley.

At the end of the service the Minister, in overcoat, scarf and gloves, leads the cortege out of the chapel and along a path to the steep graveyard. Alfred's grave has been dug high up the bank so that those carrying the coffin, including Farmer George, stumble slightly. The undertaker, a big man in a very large dark blue overcoat and oversize trousers that wobble down towards his large black boots, holds a stiff black umbrella to shelter his balding head.

DECEMBER 16TH

We drive Mother to Monmouth to see the caravan site by the edge of the river where she has decided to buy a mobile home for £3,650. It is only five minutes from the shops and everyone on the site seems friendly. "What will be will be," she says. It means we do not have to sell the Old Rectory.

I go to visit the Baileys in their new Council bungalow at Crossgates, bearing their Christmas gifts. Mrs Bailey is out shopping. Mr Bailey sits with one hand cupped to his ear as we talk. He speaks about the blessings of their forty-two years together and again he says, "Though you have been out of sight, you have never been out of mind. That great Cable has held strong." He describes the side effects of the new drugs he is taking. His eyebrows sag and he seems much frailer. He pours his tea into a saucer and sips from it, but his eyesight is not so good and he confides that often Mrs B has to say to him, "George, you've gone over the edge!"

I go to Zion Chapel for the Christmas service, which is taken by a young preacher with a shining red face, lubricious blue eyes and dark hair with gold lights in it. I nearly burst out in protest when, in his sermon, he says with such complacency, "Let us thank God that in England today – no, let us make that smaller: in Wales today; and smaller still – in Bleddfa today; let us thank God that in Bleddfa all have a house in which to worship God. Let us thank Him this afternoon that we have electricity to warm and light us, and that not one home this Christmas will be without its turkey and Christmas pudding. And let us thank God and ask him to bless these dear little children who are going to tell us the Christmas story, and let us thank God for Mrs Price who has coached them."

Having just read Michael Young's report on *Poverty in England*, especially among older people, many of whom cannot afford heating, nor other comforts, I am seething at such lack of knowledge and insensitivity.

1974

May 1ˢᵀ

My mother being settled in Monmouth, I move into what was her bedroom, but rearrange the furniture. I am apprehensive lest her loneliness, her sadness and her restlessness seep out of the walls as I sleep. But in my dreams I feel her hand on my forehead in benediction, and awake to a day of glorious sunshine.

May 10ᵀᴴ

To dinner with Dr Brian Davies and his wife, Alison. They tell me about little Fred the Flasher who lives in The Cottage, an old people's home in Knighton. He comes down at five in the morning and eats all the fag ends from the night before, and is then surprised that he has stomach trouble. Almost seventy, and only four foot tall, he's always smartly dressed, wears boots and gaiters, an anorak and a peak cap, sports a buttonhole in his lapel and carries a walking stick. Bright and inquisitive, he has a cheery word for everyone.

Maundy Thursday

The snow zooms in like crowds of white bumble-bees.

It twirls and tumbles down. Oh, the peace of the Old Rectory, its blessedness. I cook a casserole in my hay box, and a ginger cake full of fruit, cherries and nuts. As dusk falls there is a blueness reflected from the snow.

SEPTEMBER 30ᵀᴴ

Hywel and I drive to Monmouth to visit Mother in her new mobile home. On our way back, near Lyonshall, we pass a twenty-foot-high yew hedge with, on the top, a topiaried squirrel and aeroplane. Leaning out of a small upstairs window, an elderly woman watches us. We wave and she comes down to speak to us. "I thought you might have gone by the time I got down," she says. "I can't hurry. It's arthritis and rheumatism." Her white hair is thin and worn like a cap under a net. There is a long cord threaded through the end of her walking stick – "so I can slip it over my wrist when I'm getting the washing in off the line."

Her husband appears, wearing a suit, waistcoat and cap. The yew hedge, he tells us, is hundreds of years old, and is in fact two yews, one male, one female. When they first came to live here it spread its branches all over the house and over the road. "People used to shelter under it. I lopped it and trimmed it into shape and started the topiary in 1946. Why the aeroplane? That was because both our sons were in the Air Force. Those two figures are now in their prime."

His wife says she threatens to have them removed. "It scares me every time I see him go up so high on a ladder to trim them."

"They say you need only trim yew once a year," he says, "but I say give it a trim in May and again in August, cut really close. It's quite firm at the top there. You can stand on it."

"I always go into the house when he does that!" laughs his wife.

"People come from all over the world to see it and photograph it," he informs us proudly.

Hywel and I are reminded of the time we visited Powys Castle with its great battlements and walls of yew. We were sitting on a bench inside a yew hedge, when Hywel said, "I love yew," and I replied, "I love yew too." Then Hywel added: "I want lots of yew in the garden of the Old Rectory. I can't have enough of yew."

Hearing people passing by on the other side of the hedge, we suddenly realised how puzzled they must have been by our conversation!

I purchase twenty-four bottling jars and successfully bottle twelve with gooseberries, and now prepare to make blackcurrant jam.

OCTOBER 29TH

At the instigation of the Rector I conduct a day's meditation retreat at the Old Rectory for five local clergy. I light a fire in every room so that at one point each is able to go to a room and meditate for an hour.

OCTOBER 30TH

I review a batch of children's books and then pick apples

in between showers. Late in the afternoon there is a loud chink-chinking of blackbirds chiding an owl in the big tree.

NOVEMBER 13TH

I organise a concert in the church by the Craven Arms Male Voice Choir to launch the appeal for the re-ordering of the building, and to unveil our scheme. In a short speech I say that though we are few we have but to reach out our hands and other hands will come to join ours in an ever-growing circle of friendship. We end the concert by all singing "We shall overcome".

In George Pace's scheme all the Victorian pews are to be removed so that there can be flexible seating. This work is now set in progress and we find that the pews are all standing on bare earth, as a result of which a great part of the floor of the building has to be flag-stoned. In addition, the building requires rewiring, and the local bee examiner, Phil Jennings, undertakes to do this for nothing as his contribution.

DECEMBER 1ST

My mother, as might have been expected, soon feels cut off living in Monmouth and has returned for the time being to the Old Rectory, but she has her eye on a council bungalow at Crossgates where Mr and Mrs Bailey now live.

It seems that she has moved into a period of calm and quiet contentment, and instinctively avoids those things over which she would once have brooded. She takes a great interest in what is happening in the church next door, often wandering over to see how everything is progressing. She reads a daily paper and is absorbed in Sandy Wilson's autobiography.

DECEMBER 9TH

Countless letters have been sent to various foundations and individuals to raise money for the work on the re-ordering the church. In between I try to work at the seventh and last volume of the *Odd and Elsewhere* books. While shaving this morning I heard a drip-drip and turned to see one of the ceiling tiles loose and rain dripping down. I got out the extending ladder and climbed perilously up onto the roof to sweep away muck from under the duckboards and see where the rain was coming in. As I went to descend so the ladder started to swing away and I only just managed to grab hold of the guttering in time and get the ladder back into position! It was a scary moment. I have rung Mr Trillo, who has promised to come later today.

CHRISTMAS DAY

Mother is seated with the Shetland rug that Hywel gave her around her shoulders, a box of Black Magic chocolates on her lap, listening to her new radio. "It's like being in a box at the theatre!" she declares. A peaceful, blessed day.

1975

Ivan Smith comes to dinner at the Old Rectory to discuss making a crucifix for Bleddfa church.

On his first visit to the church he was deeply moved by the rafter roof. "Oh, I've got to lie on my back to look at that!" he exclaimed – and he did so for several minutes!

Born in the Welsh borders at Ewyas Harold, Ivan was thirty-seven before he decided to stop teaching carpentry and set up on his own. It was he who designed and made the large candle-holders for Stanbrook Abbey. He tells of George Roberts, the blacksmith of Llanfairfechan, "a king of smiths who would refer to a prism as the sunlit wing of a fly".

His speech is encrusted with words that are not quite modern. Looking at one of our kitchen chairs he observes, "There is a directness and a robustness, a comeliness about this chair. You see how it has an elm seat but beech sticks at the back. It is the kind of Windsor chair old Fred Lambert would make. The old ones knew where in the hedgerows to go."

At Cefn-y-Bedd, near Ruthin, he says there is a ready-made collection of old tools all boxed up to go to a museum. Could we, he suggests, make an exhibition of the tools and tackle of a farm and farmhouse to display at Bleddfa? "The iron work that interests me is primitive and agricultural. It comes out of the soil: old hinges, a latch key, a rivet forge, a door hinge, things as common as that, things a blacksmith would make just like that, but all disappearing unless someone saves them."

He often quotes from Eliot, Graves, Pound, and says of the crucifix we have been discussing for St Mary Magdalene's at Bleddfa: "That crucifix has really stretched me. I've had to unlearn, go against the mathematical formalism of what is fashionable, put myself into it. I've been reading the Bible again, how the Veil of the Temple was cleft in twain at the moment of the crucifixion."

We have decided that the crucifix has to be eleven feet high, almost to the top of the east window, dominating the church. He talks about the Zen quality of concentration needed in this kind of work, of identification with the wood, metal and stone, so that the artist and his materials are fused. "You have to make a commitment. How you travel is as important as where you travel to. If only young apprentices would learn just by being there. 'Are you watching then, lad?' says the blacksmith. If only they would bend themselves to it!"

MAY 23 RD

Breakfast, lunch and tea out of doors at the Old Rectory with Mother. The long, damp grass is mottled with moving shadows under the apple trees, with their clusters of cream and pink buds and pale green leaves. Heavy bumblebees, laden with bags of pollen, stumble among the flowers of the ceanothus, which flare up the front of the house like blue flames. Through binoculars we watch young blackbirds and thrushes on the lawn, the way they run zigzag, then pause, heads up, cocked to one side, listening, then dart forward to gobble a worm. Then, once again, they dart forward and freeze, ear to the ground, listening.

On Saturday I go to a beekeeping class in Llandrindod. This week, instead of being stung on the lip, I am stung in an earhole, the bee zuzzing inside, unable to get out. Tim, aged eight, also gets stung and his ruddy cheeks go pale. His father has net curtains around his face, topped by a brightly feathered porkpie hat of brown corduroy. He has made a hole in the net so that he can smoke.

On the way back I collect Mother who is visiting the Baileys at Crossgates. Mr B's blue eyes are fading like his hearing. He won't use the expensive hearing aids the NHS has given him as they pick up extraneous noises. He misses being able to read or write letters "but memory is a wonderful thing and through memory I am led into remembrance and thence into prayer, and in that way I feel I am able to help others."

JULY 8TH

Mother has finally got a council bungalow at Crossgates, three doors along from the Baileys.

JULY 27TH

More letters to raise money for the work on the church. I also send out leaflets about this summer's programme of workshops, concerts and exhibitions. Roger Capps, of Capps and Capps from Hay-on-Wye, a firm that specialises in restoring old buildings, has submitted an estimate. He has discovered that not only does one major beam inside the church need replacing but also two sets of trusses. Equally urgent, the entire main roof needs to be replaced. The wooden pegs which keep the existing slate tiles in place have all rotted so that the tiles are held together simply by inertia and could at any moment fall in an avalanche! It means the roof has to be stripped, re-battened, re-felted, and new tiles installed, each held in place with a steel pin.

In the churchyard, where Mr Watson is mowing the grass, I meet Elsie Hardwicke who is "chapel" and never comes to church. She turns to me. "It's wicked what you are doing, turning the church into a theatre!" I tell her that many churches nowadays have concerts of music and exhibitions of art, and that if it is so wrong then why has the Dean of Westminster, Eric Carpenter, sent a donation?

"He doesn't know what is going on! It's wicked what you are doing. The church belongs to the parish!" Mr Watson, church warden, now steps forward to defend me, but she denies that the church has to be re-roofed because rain is coming in. "There is only one tile off!" she shouts. She will not accept Roger Capps' report that the tiles are held on by inertia.

JULY 30TH

The Theatre of Puppets performs in the church, followed by the Claydon Ensemble. 145 people turn up for the puppets and just over a hundred for the concert. But it has been a week of relentless grind for Hywel and myself, having to drive to Whitton to collect folding chairs, to Presteigne for a platform, and returning all these the next day, as well as spending Saturday in Knighton at a stall, selling tickets. And rehearsals start on Monday in London for a production of *Romeo and Juliet*!

Ossian Ellis, Léon Goossens, and the York Winds of Toronto have also come to give recitals, to help raise funds. During Ossian Ellis's performance a bat flew straight at him and, to great applause, he caught it with a cushion!

OCTOBER 16TH

I call in at Caroline Gourlay's and find their middle son, aged seven, seated on the table swinging his legs.

"What's your name?" I ask.

He turns his mauve-blue eyes towards me.

"They call me Zebedee!"

He and his younger brother, Justin, come to tea at the Old Rectory. Justin rides on the rocking horse in my study, watching his reflection in the large mirror. They ask to try my yeast tablets. "Ugh!" says Justin, spitting them out. "They taste like green pepper. Ugh!"

I take them for a drive up in the forest. Justin talks of ghosts.

I nod and wave as to an imaginary ghost.

"Was that one?" he asks.

"Always wave and nod," I say, "and then it's all right."

He waves and nods, part believing me, part frightened.

"It's not a ghost, really, not really?"

"No, it's only pretend," I reply. But we go on nodding and waving just in case.

"Not so fast!" shouts Justin, for I have already told them that this is a very ancient car, called Twenty-Two Misfortunes, and that after every twenty-two miles it has a misfortune.

We get out of the car and climb up to Rhiew Pool, and Zebedee walks on a fallen tree across the pool while Justin watches apprehensively. Once Zeb has got to the other side he shouts "Now me! My turn!" I watch lest he fall and then they both insist that I also do it. Needless to say, it is I who fall into the icy water!

Justin pulls down his trousers to have a wee and makes a spurting fountain. Zeb follows his example.

"You'll flood the valley!" I say, and then they prod the pool with sticks to see if they have raised the level!

Back at the Old Rectory Zeb has so many spoonfuls of sugar that he says he should have asked for a cup of sugar with three spoonfuls of tea. Justin pours his tea into a saucer and gets down on the floor to lap it up like a dog. He starts to eat a rock cake and then spurts it out at me, laughing hysterically. I drag him away and he lies on the floor, giggling uncontrollably. At that moment, just as I'm about to mock strangle him, Caroline, his mother, arrives, and I am rescued!

NOVEMBER 10TH

The eve of my forty-ninth birthday and I walk in the hills for five hours, following the old drovers' track.

1977

APRIL 6ᵀᴴ

I telephone Marion Chesshire at the Milebrook Hotel outside Knighton. "I'm overwhelmed by daffodils," she sighs, then adds, "I'll ring you back: there's someone at the door. More trade!"

Each year she puts up a sign saying *Daffodils for Sale.*

APRIL 7ᵀᴴ

Hywel and I are driven by Jack Hollins to have lunch with Henry, the Marquess of Anglesey, at his stately home, Plas Newydd, to discuss setting up a national organisation to preserve historic churches in Wales.

"I'm willing to be Chairman," he says, "but you will find me a broken reed."

"Better a broken reed than none!" I reply.

We are to meet again in June with Ivor Bulmer-Thomas, the founder of Friends of Friendless Churches, and with the Archbishop of Wales.

APRIL 8ᵀᴴ

Hywel comes in to wake me. He draws back the curtains, saying, "See what's outside!"

It is snowing, the flakes hurtling down like a swarm of bees.

EASTER SATURDAY

Hywel and I drive to the twin-naved church of Saint Cosmo and Saint Damian, a redundant church near Pembridge, where our priest friend, John Hencher, is to lead a special Easter meditation. The church stands next to a farm and we make our way by torchlight through the farmyard and then into the churchyard. John Hencher, in a white robe, greets us at the door.

We enter the dark space, lit only by three candles, and sit on pews that have been arranged against the walls, leaving the centre space clear. Eventually, when everyone has arrived – there are eighteen of us in all – the candles are blown out and John invites us to join in the celebration of Easter "as people have been doing in this church for a thousand years, and probably longer". He leads us in a meditation on darkness: the darkness of this building, the darkness of fear, of bereavement, of disgrace; as well as the darkness within ourselves. And he asks us to join all this with the darkness in Ireland, in South Africa, in the world.

He reads the poem by Alice Meynell: "Alone, alone, alone, He rises in the darkness behind the stone."

John now goes out of the building and re-enters carrying a lit candle. Moving silently in stockinged feet, he goes up to the stone altar where he stoops with his candle by a metal trough. Suddenly a wall of flame leaps up from the trough and he proclaims, "Christ is risen!" And we reply, "He is risen indeed!"

He brings a basket of candles, which he distributes, and we each light our own, saying as we do so, "Christ is risen!"

John invites us now to consider the light that has entered the darkness, the light that will burn in our hearts until we die. I enter into the stillness, the gentleness, the heart of the flame, and think of Pauline Jobson seated next to me, in her bereavement since her husband died.

We are then invited to stand in a circle with our candles while another poem is read: one by Gerard Manley Hopkins on Easter, with its phrase "the threshold of light". At the end we lift up our candles and say again, "Christ is risen!" We embrace each other, saying "Happy Easter!" and walk about the building, arm in arm, and then out into the night, still bearing our candles.

I call out to the farmer's wife "Happy Easter!" and she replies through the darkness, "Wasn't it lovely? I've never been to a service like that!"

Back at the home of John and his partner John Cupper we are served a splendid meal. The beams of their Tudor house are like ancient ship's timbers, polished like the furniture and gleaming in the light. There is something extraordinary about this border country and the kind of people who live here, like the gathering of the light in Susan Cooper's book, *The Dark is Rising*.

I come away reflecting that we need to rethink the meaning of the word "community" in connection with rural areas. It should be apparent that in many areas of the country the old unity of a village or a hamlet is already a thing of the past. The increasing closure of churches and chapels – the incumbent pastor often having to minister to eight or even ten parishes – plus the closure of many village schools and the drift of younger people to towns and urbanised areas where there is a greater chance of employment, and the gradual disappearance of the small farmer, have had the effect of debilitating many rural areas. It may be that future governments will arrest and divert this movement, but at present there is little sign of this. If a village, especially a small one like Bleddfa, is to survive in the twenty-first century, it will have to redefine the meaning of the word "community", and each will be forced to find its own solution in pragmatic fashion. There is a Buddhist saying: "Look to the ground on which you stand." And another which says, "The journey of a thousand miles begins on your own doorstep."

APRIL 14TH

As a result, perhaps, of all the work at Bleddfa, and pondering the role of the priest in community, John Hencher says to me, "James, why don't you take Holy Orders?" Meaning, "why don't you become ordained?" While I understand at one level what he is saying I am also quite clear that I am not meant to give up my work in the theatre.

He explains about the non-stipendiary ministry, a new experiment in the Anglican church, comparable to the worker priests in France: a group that includes stockbrokers, farmers, teachers, doctors, and others who continue to earn a living like other people but who, as a result, are often more able to function in a priestly way at the margins of society. It is something to ponder.

APRIL 18ᵀᴴ

Back from Cambridge where I have directed a version of Samuel Beckett's play *Come and Go*, using five casts simultaneously, and creating the costumes and décor from newspapers and sellotape.

I start work on a special *Songs of Praise* for Bleddfa Church with a visiting boys' choir and a sermon preached by John Hencher.

SEPTEMBER 17ᵀᴴ

To Hereford, where I spend nearly three hours with Canon Murray Irving, Director of Ordinands for the diocese. I tell him that I'm not even sure I have a vocation, that I often find the word "God" a stumbling block. He laughs and says, "Most people who come to me think they are God's gift to the Church! So it is refreshing to find someone who has doubts. Also, the important thing is to realise that the church itself has a lot of dying to do."

SEPTEMBER 30ᵀᴴ

On a wild and windy day Caroline Gourlay drives me along steep twisting lanes until we arrive at Llanerchwen, up in the hills above Brecon. Here, an Anglican priest, David Shapland, and his wife, Julie, have founded a centre for priests, monks and nuns, from both the Anglican and Roman Church, who are having vocational crises.

I discuss with David Shapland my uncertainty about ordination. Might it not all be an illusion? I tell him that I have asked to see him because he is someone who stands no nonsense and can be forthright. He has a reputation for seeing through people. He listens carefully and then replies without hesitation: "If I were a bishop I would ordain you now."

He suggests I return next week to meet a colleague of his, Canon Laurence Reading, "a wise old bird", who is also a close advisor to the Bishop of Hereford.

OCTOBER 12ᵀᴴ

To Llanerchwen where I have a long session with Laurence Reading, a bearded Gandalf-like figure with watchful eyes. I sense an immediate rapport. David Shapland sits in with us.

"What you are seeking," says Laurence finally, "is authority. Ordination provides authority, as well as limitations, thereby preventing inflation of the ego."

OCTOBER 19ᵀᴴ

By train to Cardiff to speak at the Oriel Bookshop. When I get to Swansea for the return journey it is to find there have been electricity cuts and the station is illuminated by gas lamps as it used to be forty years ago. The unlit train travels through the dark, rain slashing down, with long stops at tiny halts. At intervals the guard, carrying a glass of beer, says to me, "I've told the driver to stop at Dolau for you," but when we get there the train goes shooting past. I bang on the driver's door and he at once stops the train, and reverses it back to the station!

NOVEMBER 10TH

The eve of my fiftieth birthday and once again I go walking up in the hills in the wind, mist and rain. Tomorrow, Hywel arrives from London. Tonight, while saying Compline, I am struck by the words, "He has put into my heart a marvellous love."

NOVEMBER 13TH

Mother rings in panic, thinking she has lost her social security cheque. I drive over and find her lying on her bed, her eyes red. I find the cheque at once, brew a pot of tea and make her laugh. "There's little things get in this place," she says, "and cause mischief!"

NOVEMBER 14TH

The wild weather – wind, rain and hail – continues. My car is in such a state, with rain coming in and even flooding the interior, that Mother gives me £2000 to buy a new vehicle, saying "I didn't give you anything for your fiftieth birthday."

CHRISTMAS DAY

Looking out of my bedroom window I see two cock

pheasants on the lawn, stepping delicately like a couple of eighteenth-century parsons deep in discourse, accompanied by two dilapidated looking peahens. Towards dusk Hywel sees them fly up into an ivy-mantled tree to roost.

It has been a day of recovery and thanksgiving after the excitements of yesterday.

On Christmas mornings past the congregation in Bleddfa church would swell from four to seven. So Hywel suggested that if on Christmas Eve there could be a simple service of readings and carols, the church would attract more people; because, he said, Christmas Eve is a threshold time when people often feel lonely, the children having grown up or gone away, a partner having died and so on. The Rector strongly resisted this idea but I persisted until finally he said, "Oh, all right, but only so long as you organise it all, and all I have to do is give the blessing at the end!"

And so, yesterday, for the first time in many years the church was packed! Hywel and I had moved the pews back and arranged the chairs in a series of concentric circles around a manger filled with straw. Once everyone was assembled I switched off the lights and we sat in darkness, reflecting on the words: *The people that dwelt in darkness have seen a great light.*

Then there was heard from the village green a banging of drums, clashing of cymbals, and the raucous voices of the children approaching singing *Gloria in excelsis Deo!* Outside the porch they came to a halt and we could hear a nervous muffled giggling, followed by a loud knock at the door.

"Who is it?" I called out.

"It is the Christ child!"

"Let the Christ child enter!"

The doors were opened and the children entered two by two, carrying candles and singing "O come all ye faithful!", some carrying baskets of candles, or of mince pies, while the last two, brother and sister, carried the replica of a newborn male child which they placed in the manger. Candles were distributed to everyone and lit, forming many circles of light.

And so the simple service of readings and carols and meditation proceeded, with the Rector giving the blessing of the end.

What was most revealing was that, as mince pies and coffee were handed around – in itself something unheard of hitherto – people began to move about, chatting, in small groups. No one wanted to leave and they all stayed for well over an hour. It was a real sense of community, of being together on a winter's night in a warm and safe place, celebrating the Festival of Light in the surrounding darkness.

1978

JANUARY 13TH

Mother telephones. She is in some distress as she thinks she has been robbed. Mr Bailey has died and Mother is going to church with Mrs Bailey tomorrow.

MARCH 1ST

Hywel and I drive to Bleddfa to deal with the flood. Water has burst from the tanks in the attic and into the kitchen and scullery. Mr Trillo comes and spends the whole day running up and down stairs, repairing seven leaks. It is all because I did not know about turning off the stopcock and draining the pipes before leaving.

We drive to Brecon to call on David and Julie Shapland at Llanerchwen and on the way back drop by to visit my mother at Crossgates. Her curtains are drawn. I go in to see Mrs Bailey, who says my mother's memory has gone and that she must not spend another winter alone.

As I leave I see that my mother's curtains are now open. She has been resting, so Hywel and I make tea for her.

MARCH 5TH

We tie up the plants battered by the wind, and then

85

collect Mother for a lunch of roast lamb. She is very bright, full of humour, now able to see and read with her new glasses.

MARCH 10TH?

Hywel and I drive from Bleddfa to Anglesey for a meeting at Plas Newydd with the Archbishop of Wales, Gwilym Williams; the Archdeacon of Bangor; W. R. Jones of the Representative Body; Ivor Bulmer-Thomas, founder of the Friends of Friendless Churches, and Henry Anglesey. Ivor Bulmer Thomas offers a gift of £1000 for the work at Bleddfa.

We then drive back to London.

APRIL 18TH

To the Bishop's Palace in Hereford to meet Bishop John Eastaugh and discuss the possibility of my ordination. His secretary ushers me into the library where a large marmalade cat sprawls luxuriously before the gas fire. I sit on the floor and talk to the cat, recalling how, when I was a student at Oxford I had a marmalade cat called, rather pretentiously, Cardinal Newman, which used to travel with me on my lap on the coach to and from London.

The Bishop enters, wearing a rose pink cassock with a silver cross on a chain. He sits on a sofa covered with chintz and purple cushions and inserts a cigarette into a holder which he holds with elegant fingers propped against his forehead as he listens to me. Rising, suave and elegant, to pour us each a large gin and tonic, he gossips about the theatre, so that I begin to wonder when we shall get down to business.

He has been informed by both Laurence Reading and Murray Irving that I am not prepared to go to a theological college, but this appears not to faze him. He suggests that I visit Brother Alban, the Guardian of Glasshampton Monastery at Shrawley in Worcestershire, which is the contemplative centre for the Anglican Franciscan order, of which he, as Bishop, is the titular head. "If Brother Alban can devise a form of training for you then I will accept that. I think you'll find it an ideal setting. You will have to go before ACCM, the Church's selection board, first: there is no other way. But don't mention my plan to ACCM. I don't have to heed their advice!! I am happy to be your sponsor and to ordain you."

I cross the cathedral close to tell Canon Murray Irving all that has transpired and we sip dry sherry in his elegant, tall-windowed, first floor study.

APRIL 20TH

The track up to Glasshampton Monastery is across farmland, full of ruts, winding uphill until one sights a red-pink brick building with a clock tower in the centre: the former stables of a grand house that was burned to the ground in the last century. The buildings form a quadrangle, with a lawn in the centre and the solitary grave of Father William, who converted the place into a monastery.

I sit with Brother Alban in his small cell with its

crowded desk, books piled everywhere, and the strong smell of pipe tobacco. We talk gently and then spend an hour in the chapel, meditating in silence. After supper we return to his room. He says, "Come and be here whenever your work permits, and we shall leave you to your own devices. You and I will know when the time has come for me to say to the Bishop: he is ready to be ordained." As simple as that!

APRIL 22ND

I drive to have supper with Stella Coltman-Rogers at Stanage Castle outside Knighton. A magistrate, she is very much the Lady of the Manor. At the end of the mile-long drive I draw up in front of the castellated house from which Stella emerges, wearing a straw hat, blue jeans and a pale blue denim smock with pearls.

"I didn't have time to put the pearls back in the safe," she says, "so I thought I'd keep them on."

She is carrying a punnet with a pair of secateurs inside, and is accompanied by two boisterous dogs. We go through the woodland walk with its many evergreen trees, rhododendrons, azaleas and swathes of lily of the valley. At intervals she pauses to bellow, "George! George! Juno!" then blows the whistle that hangs on the cord round her neck, saying, "Where do you think those two have gone?"

At the end of our walk the dogs come bounding back, breathless, to roll among the bluebells. On the wide expanse of the front lawn with its archery target, looking like a large Aztec eye, there is a circular ornamental basin with a fountain, and the dogs now leap into this, splashing around, shaking themselves vigorously.

In the long, pale blue drawing room Stella shows me the Red Book of Humphry Repton with its designs for Stanage, both the house and the landscape. We wander into the library, built on the north side so that the books should not fade. I follow her along corridors and rooms full of paintings, lamps (both oil and electric) bowls and vases; then down steps, past piles of logs and lines of wellington boots, into the kitchen which has a window fifteen feet tall and eight feet wide, looking out on an orchard of cherry trees. Here we mix a salad and I make the dressing. Stella fries four salmon fishcakes. For afters there are raspberries and cream, biscuits and cheese. We carry all this on trays to the long and lofty dining room, where the centre table seats fourteen, but we sit at a small table laid for two, with windows overlooking the front lawn where we can see Charles Chesshire and his brother Michael practising archery.

Stella talks about her years as a young actress in Hollywood with Mrs Stella Patrick Campbell (after whom she was named) who had adopted her. They made two films together and then Stella understudied Katharine Cornell on Broadway in *The Barretts of Wimpole Street*.

It was on her return to London that she met and fell in love with Guy Coltman-Rogers and so gave up her acting career. Years later, when she was in New York on a visit, Edward Sheldon "who was paralysed and would lie on the sofa with bandages over his eyes, and whose parties were always the most sought-after, said to me, 'But you have been given a star role in life to play!' – and indeed it has been like that."

We sit in the darkening dining room. "This was Guy's favourite room; he'd linger over meals, not wanting to leave." Then we adjourn to the library for coffee. Stella puts more beech logs on the fire and lights the lamps. She stands before the fire, in her denim suit, one hand laid elegantly beneath her throat, like a debutante of the 1930s, but the hand – both hands – are now purple. "We are hanging on by the skin of our teeth," she says. She lives here alone, with one gardener, and a girl who occupies one end of the house. "So unlike the old days," Stella says, "when there was such a sense of community, and servants would be like close and valued friends."

JUNE 8ᵀᴴ

I now await the final hurdle of ACCM. I may well not pass whatever ingenious tests are devised to sift the sheep from the wolves. I feel a quiet confidence that it will happen, even though I continue to question whether it is all self-delusion. However, what matters, whatever the outcome, is a deepening sense of commitment and dedication to whatever life brings – which may, or may not, mean ordination, but does imply its own kind of priesthood. Who would have thought that by coming to Wales eight years ago, to this tiny hamlet, and being involved with the church and school, I would have been led along this path?

I read some words spoken to the actress Mai Zetterling by her teacher: "Trust yourself. Be true to yourself. Be open. Dare to stand up for yourself, no matter what, and dare to change. Never allow yourself to become too settled. Learn that there is no security. It is better to live in a state of impermanence then one of finality."

JUNE 16ᵀᴴ

I go for the three day ACCM test and immediately on arrival am plunged into a deep depression, wanting to drive straight back to London. There are eighteen of us being considered for ordination. We sit in a circle and are each given two minutes in which to say something about ourselves. The session is introduced by the Bishop of Sherwood, a portly, jolly, bespectacled, pipe-smoking, avuncular type, much given to telling funny stories and talking to us as though we are all children. He is the chairman for the next three days. My heart sinks.

Father David Jackson, a Mirfield father, is there to check our intellectual capacities. Then there is Dorothy Edwards, a social worker, who questions me about my sexuality. I tell her about my long relationship with Hywel.

Finally there is Father Huw Thomas, who has the ability of listening with an inner ear. When he questions me about training and I tell him about Glasshampton Monastery he tut-tuts and murmurs, "All highly irregular!" He observes that from the correspondence he has been shown everyone seems eager for me to be ordained but each is waiting for someone else to give the green light!

JUNE 19TH

I have acquired a reputation for rhetoric and so am asked to make a speech of thanks to our selectors at the end. We then go to the local pub for beer and a game of skittles. One candidate, clearly convinced I'm going to be selected, says, "When you are Dean, will you remember me?"

We shall not know the results for a week but I imagine that I shall be rejected on the grounds of being too much of a maverick. While at one level I have been stimulated by the process, I am also depressed by some of the blinkered attitudes, with everything seen from the Church's point of view.

JUNE 20TH

Back in London and I feel I am at the bottom of a well. Hywel and I have one of our recurring circular talks about my career, which seems to have ground to a halt. I begin to accept that I will not be given a theatre or a company to run, and that with each year the chances of my becoming established as a freelance director grow more remote. Should I give up theatre and concentrate on writing? Do I start teaching workshops on experimental theatre techniques in the hope that, out of these, new experimental work will grow? I don't know. I just don't know … And yet I *do* know that I have not come to the end of my creativity, so all I can do is rest in each moment, each task: whether it is writing a letter, answering the telephone, or cooking a meal. And the ministry?

Is becoming a priest an essential part of my life's development, and what connection has it to the rest of my life and work? And what form will the ministry take?

John Hencher tells me that in his letter about me to ACCM he said that whatever form my ministry took it would be unorthodox, unlike anyone else's. And now he says to me, "My advice to you is to take one step at a time. Don't try to see the end of the journey. It's very tempting, especially as one gets older, when there is a greater urgency and sense of the brevity of time. You will be led each step of the way, and with each step there will be a chance to say no."

A letter arrives saying I have been accepted by ACCM.

December 20th

There is a thick frost and all the trees are delicately blanched. This evening is the children's Christmas Party in the village school and I have been asked to be Father Christmas, though the children are not to know. I have bought a special Santa costume and have wedged a pillow inside my trousers to make a paunch. I put on some make-up, then stick on a large white silky beard and moustaches, whiten my eyebrows, and sprinkle talcum on my spectacles to make them look snowed on, but also in part to conceal my eyes, for it is the eyes that reveal who one is.

Once it is dark, Peter Banks, a local farmer, and his wife Angela, arrive with a horse that has been decked out with tinsel and fitted with golden reindeer antlers that Angela has made. We load the horse with five sacks, which I have labelled with the names of adjoining villages: Dolau, Llanbister, Llandegley and Pen-y-bont. The sack marked "Bleddfa" has a small Christmas tree and a teddy bear protruding from it.

We move slowly down the lane in the dark, thick mist swirling. It is freezing and every now and then the horse slips on the ice. I hold a lantern in one hand and a shepherd's crook in the other. The children are lined up outside the school, peering through the darkness and mist as they hear the jingling of the horse's harness bells. They gaze with wide eyes as we materialise out of the mist. Asking one of the boys to tether the horse, I enter the schoolroom which is crammed not only with children but most of the occupants of the village.

"I nearly didn't get here," I say. "My reindeer broke down this morning. I know what you're thinking: how can a reindeer break down? Well, this is no ordinary reindeer. It's a sort of helicopter I have invented with a reindeer's antlers at the front. It's so that I can fly down onto rooftops and it saves a lot of time. But this morning it wouldn't work so I telephoned Mr Shaw, the Mayor of Knighton.

"Are you Shaw?" I asked.

"Of course I'm sure!" he replied.

"No, no, I mean are you sure you're Shaw?"

And he said, "Who are you?" and I replied, "It's Christmas here."

"Well, it's not Christmas here yet!" he answered.

"No, no, I mean I am Father Christmas!"

"Oh, get off the phone, you silly old man! I haven't got time for practical jokes!"

"Now look here," I replied. "I am Father Christmas and if you don't listen to me I shan't come and distribute presents on Christmas Eve in Knighton!" Well, that calmed him down!

"Well, what can I do for you?" he asked, more politely this time. So I told him I needed a horse – and here I am, as you see.

"Well, now, thank you for all your letters and I'm glad to see you are all so well, yes indeed, but now I must get on my way, because I've got all the children at Dolau and Pen-y-Bont to call on yet" – and with that I begin dragging the sack marked Bleddfa, with all their presents in, and make my way to the door.

"BUT YOU HAVEN'T GIVEN US OUR PRESENTS!" shout all the children.

"Oh dear me, dear me, how forgetful I am becoming! Now, which village am I in – is this Llanbister?"

At once there are shouts of "BLEDDFA!" from the adults as well as the children.

The first present is for Ivor Hergest, the blacksmith, aged seventy. "Oh Ivor," I say, to much laughter and applause, "you're getting a bit big for presents!" And then, turning to Mr Watson I add, "Now then, John Watson, don't get impatient! I'll be coming to you presently."

At one point I pretend to fall asleep and when all the children shout "Reindeer!" I pretend to wake up, saying, "What's that you're saying: it's raining here?"

Gradually I dole out the presents, muttering, "Where's my mince pie? I want my mince pie! I was told I would have a mince pie if I came. That's the only reason I came!"

Finally the Rector calls for Three Cheers. "And again, LOUDER!" and as I leave I can hear the children starting to sing carols.

DECEMBER 21ST

I go to collect Mother from Crossgates to come and spend Christmas at the Old Rectory. I find her seated in front of the fire, wrapped in coats, and with a scarf around her head.

"I'm taking you now," I say. "Come on, let's pack your things."

Back at the Old Rectory she retires to bed having put on two vests, a nightdress, and her dressing gown, and wrapped a scarf about her head, before snuggling down under the blankets. "I'll soon be asleep," she says.

About eleven thirty, as I'm going to bed, I hear her saying, "Oh it's so cold!" I go in to find she has removed most of the blankets because they were too heavy.

The next morning there is deep snow. Mother, on waking, cries, "Oh, I wish I could die!" I take her a cooked breakfast, then drive in to Worcester to collect Hywel off the train. This afternoon and evening Mother is more alert and plays three games of draughts, eats two meals, and when she takes a bath I can hear her singing.

CHRISTMAS DAY

Mother does not come down until twelve thirty. She sleeps and sleeps. Her feet, hands and forehead are cold, although her temperature is 94°. But she eats a good lunch, drinks champagne with her presents, and seems happy.

BOXING DAY

I sense a desire in Mother to let go, to die. She grows weary of sitting in a chair, and although I walk her around the garden and we play draughts she seems to have lost interest.

DECEMBER 27TH

Mother remains in her bedroom all day, sometimes perched fragilely on the edge of the bed, not quite sure where she is. She says she is itchy all over, and so I telephone Dr Davies who comes over straight away. He says her lungs and blood are good, "but of course she's been a borderline heart failure case since the stroke. The itching could be the kidneys failing. Basically it's the body wearing out, but there's no need for her to go into hospital."

We agree, as does Mother, that the time has come for her to be in an old people's home, with company and regular meals, and a room to herself.

I hold and cradle her in my arms after she has had supper, and she says, "Before you were born we wanted a girl. Well, you haven't done too badly!"

I laugh and say, "What a thing to say to a man of 51!"

"I don't know what I would have done without you," she says, holding me more tightly.

Then, as I leave her room after saying goodnight, she suddenly sits up in bed, sprightly as a young girl, laughing, with arms outstretched. "Good night, my darling, and thank you for everything!"

December 28th

Hywel says, "Your mother looks very white. She's obviously in distress."

"I feel that if only I could go to hospital everything will be alright," says Mother, and so again I ring Dr Davies and say she is in no state to go back to Crossgates or to look after herself: "Is there is any chance of a bed in the hospital?" Five minutes later he rings back to say there is a bed, and so I drive into Llandrindod and say to the Matron, "I think she has come in to die."

December 29th

When I call by, Mother is looking more contented, sitting up in bed with a lace-trimmed flowery nightdress. She appears rested and cheerful, having had communion, then eaten lunch. We have tea together. I tell her that I will be down on January 9th and then we will talk with Social Services.

There are warnings about a possible snow blizzard, snowdrifts and severe ice. Hywel and I drive back to London.

1979

January 3ʳᵈ

Dr Davies rings to say Mother has had a stroke down her left side but that there is no need to come yet. "She has vomited a lot and is confused. She wouldn't know you if you came."

I reply, "But I want to be with her when she dies." He promises to let me know.

Feast of the Epiphany

At one thirty Dr Davies rings to say that Mother's condition in the last twelve hours has deteriorated rapidly and to come now. Ten minutes later, just as Hywel and I are about to leave, he rings to say she has already gone.

Hywel leaves me alone. I meditate, and then open my journal at my Mother's last words to me: "Good night, my darling, and thank you for everything!"

January 9ᵀᴴ

I drive to Wales on my own. All the snow has melted and there is colour and freshness everywhere. I recite the *Salve Regina* as I drive. There is a sense of serenity about my mother's passing, even though there is an ache in my heart and a profound inner fatigue.

JANUARY 10TH

More snow, and a deeper awareness of emptiness. This is not for my mother but due to the sense of being now on my own. I die with her, and yet with her I am in the process of being born into a new life. I like Zebedee's words to Caroline as she tucked him into bed: "Shall we pray for Mrs Roose-Evans in her new life?"

I recall how she would often tap on my study door and look in, place an egg-cup of tiny flowers on my desk, or bring in a cup of coffee, each a token of her caring.

Her greatest love was to be in the garden, out of doors, relishing the spring and summer, and hating the winter with its dark and cold. She slept a lot of late and especially those three days in bed after Christmas. Sometimes when I went into her room her hands would be curled like a child's on the pillow, smiling tenderly in her sleep, happy and contented. She didn't really want to wake up and so, at the end, after vomiting a tiny amount of fluid, she just slipped away.

JANUARY 11TH

I go for a long walk in the snow-covered hills, talking to Mother, to God, and to myself, gently weeping. Moments, memories, flow past. So many shared happinesses: sitting on the roadside waiting for Hywel to drive down from London; sitting in the lee of a hedge watching new-born lambs; scaling a small cliff when she was seventy-four and laughing like a girl. I think also of her pain, of having to let go of me, and how we had to grow out of the Oedipal bonds into a new relationship. The ties that unite us are deep and ineradicable.

JANUARY 13ᵀᴴ – THE FEAST OF THE BAPTISM OF JOHN THE BAPTIST

Noon. My mother's funeral in the Lady Chapel at Hereford Cathedral. Canon Laurence Reading takes the service and then I drive with him through thick mist to the crematorium. Afterwards, as we stand outside, we see a plume of white smoke. How swift, immediate and simple – we give this body to the elements. Laurence's eyes gaze on me deeply and with concern. Later, my mother's ashes will be interred in the garden at Bleddfa, as she wanted.

JANUARY 15ᵀᴴ

For some time now I have been in correspondence with Dame Meinrad Craighead OSB, an American artist and nun at Stanbrook Abbey in Worcestershire. It is an enclosed order of Benedictine nuns, a community I have known since my early twenties when Dr Elkisch, my Jungian analyst of long standing, first introduced me to it. Now, finally, after a lengthy correspondence, I drive to Stanbrook to meet her for the first time.

One of the cloisters has been turned into a craft gallery for Meinrad's work: the walls white-washed, and studio lights installed. Along the walls are copies of her *Word of God* posters and other examples of her art. She enters briskly in her habit, with a sweater on underneath for extra warmth, her nose pink from the cold. We sit talking non-stop for three-and-a-half hours! There are so many links we share and she observes how we meet, as it were, in midstream, not having to plough through trivia and gossip.

Two years ago her own mother died, on the Feast of the Ascension. "My whole family had been to visit me and stay for Easter. They returned home to the States and three weeks later my mother was dead. I don't think one ever recovers from the death of one's mother: the umbilical cord is broken. Everything that happened thereafter had a deeper significance, and so when you wrote to me in November I knew that something important was happening. And now at last it is your mother's death that finally brings us together."

She tells me how she came to be at Stanbrook. "I was working as an artist in Rome when I suddenly felt this call. I deliberately sought out a priest whom I did not find particularly sympathetic and I made a compact with myself that I would join whatever Order he suggested." And he, taking into account her artistic gifts, suggested Stanbrook, which among other things was famous for its printing press and the artwork of Dame Werburg.

"I came to Stanbrook prepared never to paint again, only to be surprised when, at the end of two weeks, a nun took me to a small room and said, 'The Abbess wonders, will this do?' Since then I have worked non-stop. The *Word of God* posters have been so successful, and such an obvious source of income for the community – which is not at all well off – that I have nearly been swamped by them.

"I love the early mornings and the great stream of chant that merges in the river of all the chants of all religions down the ages. After breakfast I have half an hour when I sweep the refectory. I love this too: it unites me with the simple household tasks. And then from nine thirty to twelve thirty I work in my studio. Above me is Dame Werburg's studio, and at intervals I hear this *wham*! as she drags her table round to catch the light – she is now in her seventies. I know that when she's gone I shall miss that sound!

"Walking in our gardens – we have sixteen acres inside the enclosure – I love every moment, the wonder and the awareness of each present moment, which too few grasp, the now of Zen, for life is neither past nor present but simply NOW."

JANUARY 25TH

I visit Dr Johanna Brieger, Jungian analyst, GP and homeopathic doctor. I tell her about Mother's death and the feeling I sometimes have of my stomach turning over. "A part of one's own dying," I say, to which she gently responds, "And a rebirth!"

APRIL 19TH

Mother's birthday. We plant her ashes in the garden at the Old Rectory. Brother Alban, the Guardian of Glasshampton Monastery, and two other friars arrive, as well as a group of children from the village school with their teacher, Norma Beedon, plus Caroline Gourlay and

Jean Hughes. Brother Peter reads a short lesson. Brother Jeremy says a few prayers, and then on his guitar leads us in singing an Orthodox hymn for the departed, while I lower the casket into the hole that Hywel and I have prepared on the bank. Brother Alban sprinkles it with earth, makes the sign of the cross, and says a prayer, after which we have a short silence in which we can hear a lark singing, while birds swoop and dart all around us.

I then return to Glasshampton Monastery.

MAY 15TH

Jerzy Peterkiewicz, the Polish poet and writer, who was chosen by Pope John Paul II to translate his poems into English, arrives in Bleddfa to give a special rendering of the Pope's poems: he reading them in Polish and I in English. We hang a huge, twenty-foot-long wooden cross from the beams of Bleddfa church, with a posy of flowers fixed to its base, to provide a background to the performance. The two bells of the church are tolled and, as everyone assembles, the Hymn of the Virgin is played, and Jerzy and I enter carrying candles. We stop before the great cross, bow to it, then to each other. I then hand my candle to Jerzy, who ascends the pulpit, placing the candles in two holders. At the end of the performance I invite everyone to light their candles while we have a short meditation. Then we all stand to hear, on tape, the Pope's blessing to the world. Many are deeply moved.

I first met Jerzy when I adapted for radio his book *The Third Adam*, about the Mariavites in Poland. He told me how, when he had his gall-bladder removed, he was very ill. He could not eat, and got thinner and thinner. He saw various consultants but none could help and then, finally, he went to see the famous faith healer, Harry Edwards, who was then not only retired but dying. Harry Edwards laid his hands on him and said, "Spiritually you are in very good condition. You will be alright."

For forty eight hours Jerzy felt a burning sensation where his hands had been and then slowly, and from that moment, he began to get better. "I think," said Jerzy, "he changed the direction of the body's energies so that they began to work for and not against."

MAY 16TH

We drive to Stanbrook to repeat the performance for the community in the Abbey church. Afterwards, in the large parlour, the community ask many questions, such as "What colour are the Pope's eyes?"

JUNE 28TH

Glasshampton. I rise at six in the morning to say Office, then sit in the garden, the day promising great heat. After breakfast, while we wash up, I have a long talk with Bishop Bill (now in his seventies) who for fifteen years lived in an ashram in India before being appointed Bishop of Bombay.

In the early mornings and in the evenings I see him in his long black cassock, his bare, empurpled feet in sandals, seated cross-legged in meditation beneath a tree, looking across the valley. At such moments there seems to be a halo of light about this place, a holy emptiness, when everything seems to flow together, to be suspended in silence.

JULY 6TH

I drive to Port Talbot for two days of storytelling at the Aberafan Shopping Centre, staying overnight at the Bear Inn in Cowbridge. Inside the shopping centre I am overwhelmed by the size and, above all, by the noise, so that I have to shout in order to be heard. It is an impossible place in which to tell stories to children. At the end of the first day I drop by the manager's office to report. She sits at her desk frowning, clutching an enormous teddy bear on her lap, her hands clasped around its stomach. It is to be the prize for Saturday's Best Dressed Teddy Bear competition.

Sue, an assistant, enters. "We must dress him!" she declares. They take one of the International Year of the Child T-shirts and together force the bear into it. The bear sprawls as they push and pull its bulging arms through the sleeves. It looks more like the Rape of the Teddy Bear!

Later, at the hotel, over a large gin and tonic, Sue tells me that children who come to the shopping centre are dumped there during the holidays by their mothers. She then says, with all the intensity of Margaret Thatcher, "You see, these children are the next generation of shoppers. That is why you must catch them young. All life is promotion."

Driving to Port Talbot I had noticed a signpost saying: "Bethlehem – four miles". I think, "I will go there on my way back." But on the return journey I am anxious to get home, and it is already late, so I never get to Bethlehem: a subject for a sermon!

JULY 25TH

Back from teaching a theatre course in Michigan. Jean Thomas and her mother Ruth appear with shining faces to tell us what a marvellous job Roger Capps of Capps and Capps has done on the restoration of Bleddfa church, and that the Bleddfa Trust is also to receive a grant of £50,000 towards half of the cost from the Historic Buildings Council for Wales, thanks to Henry Anglesey, its Chairman. A local woman says I must hand back the money as I have no hope of raising the rest, while her husband refers to me as a passing meteor! Little does she know of my ability to raise money. I write hundreds more letters and the money comes in.

I call on Dai Evans, whose mother befriended my mother.

"Is that you, James?" He comes out as I appear at the back door.

"How did you know it was me?" I ask.

"Why, it's Lassie here," he replies, spooning some steak out of the tin into a small saucepan on the stove. "She do bark at everyone else but you. There's real fond of you she is."

Lassie, tantalised by the smell of the steak, breaks away

to nuzzle into me, clambering up me, her paws on my chest, her tail wagging, and almost pushing me over! I sit on a chair, fondling her ears.

"I was just going to have my dinner," says Dai, emptying the steak onto a plate. "Want to join me?"

"I've only just had a late breakfast. I am still feeling the effects of jetlag."

I look across at Dai's worn and earth-stained face, dark with a two-day stubble, and with eyes of the palest blue. It is the face of a mole emerging from below ground, its pale eyes blinking in the sunlight. Once a week, on market days, Dai washes, shaves, puts on a collar and tie and his one good suit.

He lifts a large old-fashioned black kettle and places it on the centre hot plate to bring it swiftly to the boil. Then, taking down two mugs from the Welsh dresser that his grandfather had when he got married, he says, "Have some coffee along o' me?"

Pouring some golden syrup into each mug he hands me one, saying "There you are, strong and sweet as my Mam always used to make it. 'It will put hairs on your chest!' she would say. Now, tell me all about your trip to America."

Later, he takes out his tobacco pouch and cigarette papers and begins to roll himself a cigarette.

"Why did you never get married, Dai?" I ask.

He goes on easing the tobacco and spreading it into the machine before he replies.

"There were one or two girls I fancied but, do you know, I scared 'em off! They thought I were mucky!" He grins. "Wanted to clean me up, I dare say, but I thought better on't."

He lifts the cigarette paper to his lips and wets the gummed edge.

"When I came back after the War I lived with our Mam. All my brothers and sisters had either married or moved away. And Dad was dead. I suppose Mam spoiled me for anyone else. Anyway, when she died last year, not long after your mother, well, I just didn't feel like living with anyone else. Women! Ha, they want to tidy you up. Then out in the morning, first thing, like them geese, and not back till nightfall! 'Wipe your shoes, hang up your coat, do this, do that, don't get under my feet!' Aye, I've seen it. And so have you. Remember old Jack Meredith up at Ty Bach? Even after he'd retired, his old missus would never let him in the house during daylight. Many's the time we found him sitting in his barn isn't it, Lass? Having a kip because she wouldn't let him in the house. Even on a wet day. Or you'd find him sitting in that old Morris of his down at the Post Office, reading the paper afore his missus got it. 'Now, don't you let on, Dai!' he would say to me. 'Else you'll get me into hot water and my life won't be worth living.' And even when they sold up and went to live in Knighton she'd push him out of the house and you'd see him hanging about the street in all weathers. No wonder he died of double pneumonia. I only hope he's in a warmer place now."

"But don't you find it lonely, sometimes, on your own here?" I persist.

He strikes the match and lights the ragged ends of

tobacco protruding from the end of his cigarette. He waits until he has got it going before answering.

"Of course it's lonely at times. But so was it for Jack and he was married! Perhaps in a way he was more lonely than I am. Lonely is part of the human condition, isn't it? But me, well, at least I have only got myself to please. I can have my supper in the middle of the night if I choose. I can go to bed with the dawn, after staying up all night doing a bit of carpentry. And do you know what I value most, James? It's having time to think. Time to think without some woman going yackety-yack all the time! Mind you, I don't mean that all women are like that, of course not. Mam wasn't, and marriage is right and good for some. But me, well, it would just be my luck, wouldn't it, to land a yacker! When you live on your own there's no-one to interrupt your thoughts. Sometimes I sit here for hours watching the birds. Yesterday, do you know, a sparrowhawk flew down to the bird table and lifted off a sparrow. And there was no one but me to see it, and I couldn't do nothing, it all happened so quickly."

"But it must get lonely sometimes?"

"Well, it's not as though I'm here all the time, is it? I'm out and about with my ladders so that I see plenty of folk. One thing about window cleaning – oh, did I tell you, I've got a contract to do John Beddoes School in Presteigne? Plenty of windows there to keep me busy! Yes, you see all sorts when you're cleaning windows. And you see things people don't see. I enjoy cleaning windows. Especially when they be finished. You can see through them! And out of 'em too! You can see so clearly you'd think there was no glass there, and yet it's the glass that protects us from the elements."

He rises, putting away his tobacco pouch, and carries the two mugs to the sink.

"No, when Mam died, everyone was saying how I should marry if only to have someone to cook and wash and darn my clothes and such like. But that didn't seem to me the right basis for a marriage. The boys down at the pub used to jest and say, 'How are you going to keep warm, Dai, on a winter's night?' And I'd answer, 'I'm going to buy me a hot water bottle!'"

SEPTEMBER 19TH

I drive to Stanbrook Abbey to spend four hours with Meinrad, who has just returned from America where her father has had a triple bypass. Both she and Sister Rosemary Davies, the bursar and longest serving member of the community, have decided to leave. Meinrad says it became quite clear to her in America that the time had come to leave Stanbrook and she was tempted not to return at all but recognised that this would have been cowardice, and also Rosemary would have been bereft.

As we are talking Rosemary enters, looking pale, with shadows under her eyes, and a pink soreness at the base of her nostrils. She warms her hands at the Calor gas stove while Meinrad makes her a cup of coffee. Rosemary is frightened of the step they are taking. She entered the Order when she was twenty-three, having done a secretarial course, and has been here twenty-one years. She is not an artist, driven by a vision like Meinrad. Yet at the same time Rosemary says, "I came here to be a contemplative, and I have ended up as bursar, dealing in stocks and shares, and issuing toilet rolls and bars of soap!"

I ask Meinrad whether she might be able to make me a crucifix for the cellar chapel at the Old Rectory in Bleddfa. "Wait there!" she says, and disappears, leaving Rosemary and me to talk quietly. When Meinrad returns she is carrying something covered with a cloth. Unwrapping it she reveals a square ceramic image, in the centre of a thick wooden cross of polished wood.

The image is of a small squat Christ figure, with large hands and feet. It is as though Christ, like a mole, is burrowing his way up through the earth towards the light: a perfect image for an underground chapel! A mole, which is nearly blind, has amazing strength and tenacity, and is capable of moving ten pounds of soil upwards in twenty minutes – the equivalent of a twelve stone miner shifting four tons! For each of us the task is the climb upwards towards greater consciousness. Like the mole we cannot see what we are doing, but we follow an innate impulse that leads us towards the light. I ask Meinrad how much it is to buy? She smiles and replies, "Dear James, it is a gift from Stanbrook!"

NOVEMBER 11TH

My fifty-second birthday. Hywel and I spend it at the Old Rectory, with Joyce Grant and Johanna Brieger as our guests. At eleven o'clock Albert Thomas arrives with Beth and Leah carrying an enormous birthday card made by all the schoolchildren. When they have gone Hywel puts on the Bach *Double Violin Concerto* which Joyce has given me. I close my eyes to listen and at some point in the music my mother "arrives", and is present with all her warmth, vitality, humour and love. Blessings seem to be descending upon my head. Mother "recognises" Joyce, sees Hywel and welcomes Johanna. The kitchen is full of presences. I discern Franz Elkisch and he is laughing. Tears pour down my face. I feel so abundantly blessed, surrounded by love. I realise in an instant that Franz and my mother are protecting me, and that they are my true parents. Then I hear whispers. It is Hywel talking quietly to Joyce about getting in the rest of the apples. Slowly I am returned to the present moment.

This year I also celebrate twenty-one years with Hywel, in a relationship that is deep rooted, in spite of many mistakes on my part. It is a friendship with many branches, still growing, still bringing forth new leaf and shedding the old.

NOVEMBER 15TH

The fight is on to save Bleddfa school from closure on account of dwindling numbers. As Correspondent for the school I begin to rally forces and call a meeting at the Old Rectory to discuss tactics.

NOVEMBER 17TH

Glasshampton. A white wall of mist envelopes the monastery. Moisture drips from the bare apple trees onto the blackened leaves that litter the wet grass. A rabbit, caught by surprise in the flower bed, lollops away. Brother Pascal emerges to place a bowl of steaming water on the bird table together with some crusts of bread. A blackbird hops across the lawn.

Afterwards I drive to Stanbrook to spend three hours with Meinrad. She speaks of her sense of the deadness of the community. "In the last ten years it has stopped growing." She speaks of the isolation at Stanbrook. "There isn't the empathy or awareness of each for the other in this community. I am so grateful for Sister Rosemary's friendship after the death of my mother."

She questions me about my being priested and how I see my ministry. And when I am ordained will I celebrate a simple Eucharist there in the craft cloister? "No one need know. There will be just Rosemary and perhaps Johanna Brieger, and then if the chaplain happens to pass by he will just think you are doing something with the teacups!"

She tells me she often hears her mother's laugh or her mother calling her by name.

NOVEMBER 20ᵀᴴ

Glasshampton. Washing up after lunch today, Brother John, now in his seventies, launches into a long story about Bob Harris who was the village policeman when he was a boy.

"He could swear like a trooper, could Bob Harris! He'd be on traffic duty in town, waving and signalling, and he'd see me and say, 'Look at that bleeding bugger there! Go down Nottingham Street, you bloody bastard!' And my mother would grab me by the hand and hurry past! 'He ought not to talk like that!' she would say.

"Now there was this man, Percy. I used to help him up by the allotments and my mother used to say, 'You shouldn't' and my dad would say 'Why not?' And she would reply, 'There's something cruel about him' – and by gum, she was right!

"What happened was this. He had an affair with the manageress of a teashop, and he married her without letting on that he was married already. He would make up stories to explain why he was always away: that he had to visit his parents in Cambridge, and so on. Well, one night, he said to his wife, 'I've bought an apple tree, it's up by the allotments. I can't plant it there because boys would only pinch the apples, so I want you to help me carry it home.' So she went up to the allotments and he hit her on the head with a spade – and she wasn't even dead, it's thought – and he buried her alive. The next day when people said, 'Where is your wife?' He replied, 'Oh, she's gone to see her mother in Cumberland for a day or two.'

"The next day, Dan Jenkins was taking a walk up along by the allotments with his dog and his patch was very near Percy's. And his small dog began scrabbling away and yelping, and Mr Jenkins went to see what the dog was up to, and there was Percy's wife staring up at him. It upset him real bad. He was off work for three months after that with shock, but he had the sense to go down to some railway cottages and leave a message for Bob Harris. The police caught Percy the next day. He always denied killing his wife but he was sentenced and hanged in Derby. And I remember Bob Harris coming down the street, walking in the middle as he always did, and shouting out, 'The bloody bugger's going to swing!' And the women coming out and cheering. I think if Percy had been let off they would have lynched him. And you can write that down and use it in one of your stories. Thank you for listening!"

NOVEMBER 30ᵀᴴ

To Glasshampton again. The chapel windows shine beetroot red. After Eucharist and before the breakfast bell, Brother David, finger to his lips, waves Brother Damien and me into his cell to observe the large red disc of the sun on the opposite hill and, silhouetted against it, an oak tree.

Then back to Bleddfa to help save the school from closing. Everyone in the village – including Miss Woosnam, aged eighty-two – packs into the school for an official meeting with the Director of Education for Powys. All the children, including several babies – the next generation of pupils! – and the local councillors, are there.

The Director smoothly tries to sweep aside my facts, and then snidely asking, "Are you a parent?" – knowing I am not – adds, "Then what right have you to speak?"

He talks about the Council's desire to confer with local people about the future. "No decision has yet been taken, but after today's Government cuts the future is more serious. There is always a lot of feeling when a school is closed, but the Local Education Authority is aware of the difficulties and recognises that a resolute approach to closure is the best."

He doubts whether small schools can attract quality teachers, and he speaks of "efficient and economic deployment. In Powys, in the last year, we have had enormous problems in making ends meet and these decisions are only just beginning. After today's Government cuts we have to find savings of £700,000. There will be an increase in rates and a reduction in services. This small school is inordinately costly. In the past we have regarded the needs of the community. There will have to be strong and ample justification of purpose at this meeting to see if there is an argument for keeping Bleddfa school open. Recently we have had here one teacher and an assistant teacher, but the latter has had to be removed. Now there is one teacher and a nursery assistant, but if she were to go, what would happen then? These are all factors that the Education Committee must consider."

Tom Nicholls, from the floor, says, "We have to have regard for those young children who would then be forced to travel long distances to get to another school." Mrs Harris, mother of ten children, with six of them present, speaks movingly of "having had children in a large school I know the benefit of a small local school. Take John here, he was off a term through no fault of his own but now, thanks to the teacher, he has caught up. And take David here, he's my grandson, he's slightly deaf, would he get the attention in a larger school that he gets here? The answer is No!"

Finally the Rector asks for a vote. Only Cliff Gittoes

abstains. Suddenly we are a village – all sorts of people meeting and talking to one another, and the children helping to pass cups of tea around. The Education Committee meets next Monday so we shall soon know the result. At least we have made a good stand.

DECEMBER 2ND

Glasshampton. Brother David has just spent three and a half days in solitude at Freeland, the convent for Franciscan nuns outside Oxford. He tells how the Sisters there put roses in his room along with bread, cheese, apples and coffee. "I had no books, but the roses became my meditation. They taught me how to grow old gracefully, how to let go, how to die. And some were buds that never developed, like some members of our Community!"

He is now the oldest living member of the Society of Saint Francis and was its first provincial Minister. Born in North Wales, he's been a priest for fifty-six years. He was a parish priest until the age of forty-five when he joined the Cowley Fathers but then went to live for two years in solitude in a cottage at Wescott, between Stowe and Burford, looking after some nuns. In the end he joined the Society of Saint Francis, which, at that time, had only thirty-four Brothers.

Although he is eighty there is very little grey in his hair, which keeps falling across his forehead in a boyish lock. Tiny, bird-like in his movements, he is extraordinarily youthful, his eyes bright and brown, his cell a model of tidiness. He takes his turn in the laundry, or at washing-up in the kitchen, and he and I spend many hours in the chapel. He sits on the chair in front of the Blessed Sacrament and I on my meditation bench at the back of the chapel. He wraps round himself a brown wool plaid blanket – "It belonged to a Scottish shepherd and is more than a hundred years old. I have had it for fifty years." He reads, prays, or falls asleep. We are aware of each other's silence, hour after hour. He is the one from whom I have learned most in our long hours of quiet together.

DECEMBER 8TH

I have been invited by the National Trust to direct a Victorian Extravaganza next year at Plas Newydd in Anglesey. It is to be for three successive nights and will be like staging an open-air production. And so I drive from Bleddfa to Anglesey, going over Dylife by the mountain route. At Machynlleth there are signs saying "The Dolgellau road is flooded" and a road sweeper advises me to "Take the chemist road." I am puzzled and eventually stop at the garage where the attendant points on my map to "Cemmaes". "You take the Cemmaes Road," he says.

I drive through Dolgellau where Hywel worked in the library after leaving school and before joining the Army, onto Porthmadog and thence to Caernarfon, and arrive to meet Elved Lewis, the National Trust regional officer for this part of Wales. Together we walk the grounds of Plas Newydd so that I can explore some of its theatrical possibilities. It is dark by the time I return, the mountain roads swirling with mist, the road twisting and turn-ing, rising and falling, and I drive too fast, anxious to be home. I am tired and must not attempt this journey twice in a day again.

Christmas week

Once again I am Father Christmas! I arrange with the schoolmistress that as soon as it is dark, someone will put up my extending ladder at the back of the school and be there, holding it, at five minutes to six, when I will arrive and climb up it onto the roof by the chimney stack, which is where the children are to find me. However, when I arrive there is no sign of anyone and the ladder is lying on the ground. From inside the school comes the loud singing of carols. I am bulging with blankets and a pillow under my costume so that I wrestle with the ladder and two sections fall apart with a great crash! I struggle to get the ladder upright but again it falls apart in two sections. I begin to sweat and my beard starts to come unstuck. The goatskin across one shoulder slips, pinioning my arms. I now carefully slide one section of the ladder into the other, and heave it up to the roof. It sways and then, because I can't control the weight, it falls with a mighty crash onto the roof. But inside nothing is heard, because the children appear now to be watching a puppet show... I hunt around and find the sacks and begin to climb up to the roof, dragging one of the sacks with me, but the ladder begins to slip sideways. I am still on it but only half way up to the roof. I cling to the guttering and bang loudly on the roof. Does anyone hear? No! I bang and bang and bang. Where the bloody hell is everyone? I shout. I am weary with banging. Suddenly

Albert appears with a powerful flash-lamp and a trickle of children, then more, all standing below, looking up at Father Christmas on the roof.

"I told you not to block up the chimney!" I cry. "And you've got the fire going – why, I might have singed my whiskers!"

Slowly I descend and enter the crowded schoolroom.

"Now, let me see, where am I? What? Bleddfa? Oh, that's where a little girl last year promised me a jar of chutney and never gave it to me. What's that? You've remembered this year? Well, I hope it's fresh! I don't want last year's chutney, you know! I'm very glad to see you all. Because we heard a rumour up in Lapland that your school was going to close. So I got on the Polar telephone and rang Mr Robert Bevan, the Director of Education for Powys.

'Now, Robert,' I said. Of course, I've known him since he was in his nappies! Gave him his first present, didn't I? 'Now, look here, Robert, you can't close Bleddfa school!'

'Why not?' he said.

'Because if you do,' I replied, 'I'll be out of a job!'

'Oh, we hadn't thought about that. I'll have to put that to the Education Committee in January. We can't have our Father Christmas out of a job!'

"Oh dear, I am tired! We no sooner get one Christmas over than I have to start planning the next. I'm getting on in years, you know. I'm not as young as I used to be. Have you any idea of how old I am, eh? Hundreds and hundreds and hundreds of years! But I tell you something, next year I'm going to have help. Mrs Christmas always says, 'Dad, why can't I come with you? I'm sure I could help.' And so I have decided that next year Mrs Christmas will be here to give me a hand. How about that! But now I must go, I've got all these other villages to visit…"

And again the children shout out, "YOU HAVEN'T GIVEN US OUR PRESENTS!"

"Oh dear, haven't I? But where's my mince pie and my jar of chutney?"

I distribute presents to the children and then to all the OAPs – and it is interesting to observe the licence one has as Father Christmas, the way all the women want to kiss one full on the lips, something they'd never do if I weren't dressed up as Santa.

The days whizz by with setting up the church for the second year of the Christmas Eve service. Ninety people this year, in spite of snow, and freezing hard. No wonder I wake up on Christmas morning, aching all over and thinking, Why do I do it?! Hywel brings me breakfast in bed and then I prepare lunch. Jack Hollins arrives, much moved by the service last night when we also had the Corndon Singers and medieval instruments.

Over lunch, Jack tells us of their family butler, Binfold. "He used to sit knitting and singing arias in a high, soft voice." Jack's dentures slip as he laughs. After lunch he pours boiling water over the engine of his car and drives off. Hywel and I then walk up to Rhiw Pool. The snow is scribed with criss-crossing lines made by the sheep. The sun, low down, fills the ruts with colour, and each sheep, as it moves, casts a long blue shadow. Across the valley the hills are white with snow, shaded with mauve.

1980

At Glasshampton, seated in the chapel before supper, I reflect on darkness. It seems to me that when we speak of evil we should avoid the words "dark" or "black", for there is a beauty in darkness that is primal and paradisal, when we sense nature at work in the earth, in rocks, rivers and oceans, in the whole universe and its mysterious nocturnal activity. The contrast of dark and light as evil and good, in both of the Hebraic and Christian traditions, is an anthropomorphic projection. Dark and light, as the Tao teaches, are inseparable aspects of Nature.

After supper, another hour in the chapel. Suddenly nine o'clock strikes: how time flies when one's concentration is withdrawn to the still centre. and lightly held. It is like bird-watching, when one remains physically very still, alert and watching. Only that in prayer one is waiting upon a Presence that is always there, even in the darkness of winter or the cloud of unknowing.

I wonder whether, as Meinrad was saying, it is the church itself as institution that has come to stand in the way of the teachings of Jesus? Perhaps we need to approach Christianity more as a faith than a religion? All faiths seem to need some form of container, some structure, which is why churches, temples, mosques and synagogues have come into being. Yet in the earliest years of Christianity there were no churches: people simply met in each other's houses. In Jesus' teaching there is no mention of bricks and mortar, only of where two or three are gathered together in his name.

Brother David, who is disillusioned by the institutionalism of the Church, says he always refuses to refer to *the Church* in prayers. He tells me, "I always say *the Family of God* or *the Body of Christ*. All mankind is God's family. For some, the way to God is by being a good Muslim or a good Hindu. I, as a Christian, naturally want to share my Christian insights with anyone who wants to come in. But we are all one family. The Body of Christ is not the external Church!"

The words that have been much on my mind these past days here at Glasshampton are, as so often, those of Eliot in *Little Gidding*. At the end of the poem, he reminds us of the need for "a condition of complete simplicity, costing not less than everything".

FEBRUARY 9TH

It is six thirty in the morning and dark as I step out into the garden and stand on the terrace overlooking the valley in the twilight of dawn. A thrush is singing, answered by another, then by a third.

My thoughts turn, as so often, to Hywel, who has arrived at a plateau of maturity and inner authority. How moving is the green freshness of youth, and the unmapped faces of the young; but there is a greater beauty in early summer into harvest, the faces mapped now with wrinkles and shadows, the body shaped by the flow of life within and without, and that sense of gravitas of the centre.

Here at Glasshampton the seasons come and go. I have known it for nearly two years now, in full summer, in snow, during the time of my mother's death, in spring, summer, autumn and now winter again. I have experienced peace and crisis here as well as growth. The words of Thomas Merton come to mind: "Fundamentally, it probably comes to this: living in silence so reconciles contradictions within us that, although they remain within us, they cease to be a problem."

FEBRUARY 10TH

A clear dawn of washed colours, a new moon, robins and blackbirds singing. During Mass a brilliant sunrise sends shafts of light through the chapel windows, emphasised by the lingering clouds of incense, as Brother David celebrates the Eucharist.

FEBRUARY 11TH

Talking in the kitchen with Brother Gregory about counselling, he tells me that friars are not trained in the skills: only to be loving, to give each person the feeling that they are the only one who matters. He describes how a boy of fourteen came to see him recently, sent by his headmaster. The boy was from a wealthy background and had got into drink, drugs and sex. He talked non-stop for an hour. Afterwards the headmaster wrote to say, "I don't know what you said to the boy but it has had an extraordinary effect upon him." As Gregory said to me, laughing "I didn't say a thing!" Clearly, however, the quality of his listening was so total that the boy was able to see himself as in a mirror.

FEBRUARY 13TH

I asked to come to a place where I might have a Zen-like preparation for the priesthood, rather than a theological college, a place of quiet, prayer, study and manual work. I have absorbed so much by being here at Glasshampton. I have learnt so much from the silence.

MARCH 9TH

London. At about eight o'clock I am woken by the telephone and hear Hywel answering it in the front room. I get up. Hywel calls and I go in. It was his brother-in-law, Jac, to say that Hywel's mother, Catherine, died last night. I lie with Hywel, holding him in the silence. After breakfast I go to the early Eucharist and ask Chit (Prebendary Ernest Chitty) to remember Hywel in his prayers. Then, at the intercessions, I hear him saying "Let us pray for Hywel and his family as they mourn the loss of their mother, and let us pray for Catherine that she may enter a place of peace, refreshment and light." I weep copiously and think how curious it is that both our mothers were named Catherine.

When I return, it is to find that Hywel has cleaned the flat, laid the table and set a white hyacinth in a circle of night lights, for the supper party to welcome our friend Joyce Grant back from South Africa.

MARCH 12ᵀᴴ

Hywel and I both wake in the night. I brew a pot of tea. His stomach has been upset for several days, and now he has diarrhoea, clear signs of his emotional disturbance. In the morning he drives off to Wales for his mother's funeral.

MARCH 16ᵀᴴ

Hywel writes to thank Sister Meinrad for her prayers: "Thank you very much for your thoughts and prayers during my mother's illness and now her sudden death. Your lovely card was here when I returned from Wales. I was shattered by the funeral, which took place in the chapel where my mother took me by the hand as a little boy, and the memory of this early relationship flared up with great force. Also the pain in my mother's life – she'd had a lot of mental illness following the birth of my youngest sister. I cried for her pain as she lay under the flowers, free from it all. I think you are right, I shall be closer to her now and her memory will remain green until I die myself. We are fortunately a close family and a great support to each other. I know from James that you have also been through difficult times. I hope very much that you will find your way to calmer waters. With much, much gratitude, Hywel."

MARCH 18TH

We drive to Wiltshire to visit Simon Verity, from whom I have commissioned a statue of Mother and Child to stand in the garden of the Old Rectory in memory of my mother. He lives with his wife and children in an old primary school near Malmesbury. Immediately on arrival he drags me into his workshop to show me the statue of Saint Peter he is working on. It is a commission for Exeter Cathedral and it will stand at the very apex. He tells me how he himself went up there, some ninety feet or so, and stood, looking out over the water-meadows.

His workshop is a death trap, cluttered with old sculptures and pieces on which he is working, and everywhere a fine film of white dust. His work seems to penetrate the whole house. Sometimes he works at the kitchen table, or goes up to sit in the bath to polish stones. He even goes to bed in the middle of the day in his dusty clothes and boots "to have a think or work away at a small piece of stone", and late at night Judith, his wife, discovers the bed is full of tiny chippings! The house has a feeling of cosy neglect, and the garden is unfinished, with the children, Polly, Thomas and John, sleeping out in a tent.

Outside, the playground is littered with chunks of stone and carvings. At the far end there is something covered with a red cloth, which Simon whips off and then runs away! He is so nervous of my reaction. But what he has done takes me happily by surprise. It is not the traditional image of a mother standing with a baby in her arms as I had envisaged. This has been carved out of four square feet of stone, and shows the child, with a child's heavy bottom, running towards the mother with arms upraised to greet her, while she is reaching down to encircle and support the naked infant. Her arms curve like a benediction and their faces meet within the circle of arms as though about to kiss, but there is a space between their faces through which one can see the sky. The mother welcomes the child but she is also setting the child free, teaching it to stand on its own feet. She is, as it were, drawing the child up to manhood. There is a feeling of rootedness, and yet also of sap flowing along branches.

JULY 5TH

Simon Verity arrives to install the statue of Mother and Child in the garden of the Old Rectory. Brother Alban brings with him from Glasshampton several of the friars for a simple ceremony. The schoolchildren, accompanied by their teacher, sing "I gave my love a baby without any crying", and I speak the anonymous poem, "My Master hath a garden, full filled with diverse flowers". Then Brother Theodore, seated cross-legged on the lawn, sings an Easter hymn, "The green blade rises"; and Brother David ends with the prayer I have written for the occasion, blessing the statue, its maker, the garden and all who enter it. The friars and I then go down to my cellar chapel to say the Midday Office and afterwards we all have lunch.

JULY 14TH

Sister Clare at Carmel in Presteigne asks me if I will see

Sister Angela. "You may be able to divert her. She is now very fragile, unable to walk, and lies much of the time on her bed in despair."

The only time I have met Sister Angela was last year when she asked to see me, having heard that I was always buying the pot-pourri sachets she made. I recall her as being like a tiny Arthur Askey, laughing, talking of wanting to die, but joking that clearly the Good Lord didn't think she was good enough yet!

This time, when she is wheeled in, her eyes seem large and serious, and she appears to be looking at me as though from a long way off. When we are left alone I kneel and hold her hands. "Is the waiting very long?" I say. And she replies, "Yes."

There is much shared silence between us, like two people clinging to a rope and no sign of the ship anywhere.

JULY 16TH

I decide to give Sister Angela a surprise. I take to Carmel the oval-shaped painted tin chest in which I store all the sachets she has made and which I have bought to give away from time to time.

When she is wheeled in by Sister Teresa, Sister Clare and two other nuns, I tell Sister Angela I've been meditating on the sentence, "Open to me the treasures of your love." I then open the chest, which is filled to the brim with the sachets she has made. Her eyes fill with tears and she says, "Did I make all those?!" Her face glows, she smiles, and seems lifted out of herself.

1981

FEBRUARY 10TH

Bishop John telephones to say he intends to go ahead and ordain me deacon at Glasshampton Monastery on March 1st, St David's Day, and will ordain me priest in the Cathedral on June 28th "to be a presence, to exercise the ministry, hidden but not secret".

FEBRUARY 27TH

I drive through a snowy landscape to Glasshampton in preparation for the diaconate on Sunday. I spend many hours in the chapel, kneeling before the great crucifix on the wall behind the altar. In prayer one is the pool, allowing the Other, which is the Transcendent, to imprint its reflection.

MARCH 2ND

The snows have all gone, and the sun shines. Mist rises, as well as clouds of midges, above snowdrops and primroses. My tinnitus continues, but I now accept its ringing in my head as a constant companion.

MARCH 3RD

I rise at three to begin a vigil in the chapel. At five, Brother Andrew enters. At six I take a bath, shave, and change into a clerical collar and cassock. I then go outside to watch the dawn. The delicate saffron and primrose yellows of the sky signal the approach of day and then I see, far down, lights slowly ascending the farm track as a chauffeur-driven white car glides into view, bearing the Bishop and Laurence Reading. Laurence holds me by the hands and gazes thoughtfully into my eyes, asking, "Everything all right?"

The Bishop carries his case along with his pastoral staff, which he slots together like a conjurer's wand.

"You've got some swearing to do first!" he says as I sign various legal papers.

Then, robed, we are finally in our places and the simple but solemn service of the ordination of a deacon commences, with the Bishop's hands pressing heavily on my head for the descent of the Holy Spirit. We sing "Guide me, O thou great Jehovah" to the tune of Cwm Rhondda, as it is St David's Day. We also sing my favourite hymn: "We love the place, O God, wherein thine honour dwells." After the giving of the Peace I go to each member of the community in turn, from Brother Alban to Brother David, and the others, as well as to Hywel, giving the kiss of Peace to each.

MAY 10TH

At Bleddfa I go to Sion Chapel. Standing outside after

the service, Mrs Powell says how pleased she always is to see my light at the Old Rectory, and Farmer John George comments, "A light is a great comfort in the country. You feel less lonely."

I compliment Miss Tilly Lloyd on her colours: new shoes, dress, coat and hat all a deep blue, echoing the blue of her eyes. She blushes like a young girl, ducking her head in a sideways motion, smiling shyly with pleasure. The other women tease her: "Nice to have compliments from a young man!"

John and Joyce George invite me to join them for tea at the farm. There is cold pork with salad, bread and butter, fairy cakes, and tea, served in the best parlour, where their daughter Elizabeth is watching television.

MAY 11TH

I invite Mrs Gwenny Powell and Miss Tilly Lloyd to tea at the Old Rectory. They sit by the fire having honeyed toast. Tilly Lloyd's face lights up each time she smiles, but always with her head tilted to one side, as though trying to avoid attracting attention. She clings to shyness and anonymity, not wanting to trouble anyone, seeking instead to slip past unnoticed, always clinging to the side of the lane or the road, always ready to wait on others, never asking anything for herself. She is like a winter lantern. She shines with goodness.

MAY 12TH

While waiting for the car to be serviced at Dolau garage I

pick a small posy of daisies and cuckoo flowers to put in front of Mother's picture, recalling how often she would leave on my desk an egg-cup full of tiny flowers.

MAY 14TH

Glasshampton, ten minutes before lunch. Birds are chattering, wheezing, carolling in the misted valley. A woodpecker is drumming away at a tree, a pheasant rattles its alarum, and cuckoos endlessly repeat themselves. Bishop Bill is seated in meditation under a pink-mauve magnolia tree.

MAY 20TH

I drive back with four white doves I have bought – named Matthew, Mark, Luke and John! I place them in the dovecote on its tall pole at the end of the garden of the Old Rectory, in the centre of the circular rose bed, and cover it with netting so that they cannot get out until they are acclimatised.

MAY 30TH

Stella Coltman-Rogers and her youngest daughter Sue, who is to marry Michael Bond, the author of the Paddington Bear books, arrive for supper at the Old Rectory. Afterwards, wrapped in eiderdowns and blankets, we sit in the dark on the hammock outside, with all the lights in the house on, so that it looks like a lantern or an Advent calendar. The four doves alight on the roof like a benediction.

"It's a happy house," says Stella.

There is indeed something very blessed about this place.

JUNE 25TH

JUNE 25TH

Back in Bleddfa. John Rowlands-Pritchard arrives, bearing a bottle of claret and the bulk of his exhibition of calligraphy. A tall, gentle person with an inner passion and fire, he is both a Lay Vicar Choral at Wells Cathedral and a calligrapher who uses rich colours as well as collage in his work.

Tomorrow I depart for the ordination retreat in Hereford.

JUNE 26TH

I arrive at the palace to find Bishop John at the back of the house, like a butler, emptying gin bottles into the bin.

All fourteen of us then troop into the cathedral for Evensong, followed by a rehearsal for the Ordination service on Sunday.

JUNE 27TH

I try to meditate in the Bishop's private chapel but the windows are open to the garden and the conversations of people outside. I go over to the cathedral in an attempt to find somewhere quiet. As I enter the cathedral I am greeted by a blare of music and the commentary from a television screen showing a film about pilgrims! I escape to the Lady Chapel where the

Blessed Sacrament is kept, but the coming and going of talkative tourists makes it difficult to focus. Observing to one side of the Lady Chapel a small chantry chapel, I try the door but it is locked, so I go to the head verger and ask if I may have a key to lock myself in there for the next two days.

This small enclosed space becomes my "desert", where I can make a proper retreat. While I can still hear the voices of tourists, and the sound of hoovers in the cathedral and drills outside, the noises are at a distance. Above the altar hangs a three-dimensional portrait, carved from wood and painted, of the Virgin and Child. There is a sturdiness about the child's sucking at the mother's teat, its hands reaching up to hold each side of the breast with a passionate intensity, and the face of the mother serene and rapt, while in the background are the silhouettes of crosses, an intimation of what lies ahead.

As I make this image the focus of my meditation, the organist begins to play Bach's *Wachet Auf*, which he played for my mother's funeral, when her coffin rested next door in the Lady Chapel.

At the end of lunch in the Palace Bishop John appears in shirt sleeves and purple stock to assist Bridget, his wife, clear the table and wash up. On the lawn, black-robed young ordinands assemble to play croquet, just as before lunch they had assembled in the drawing room with sherries and cigarettes to read *The Times* and the *Church Times*. Trollope, thou art with us still! I return to the chantry chapel for the rest of the afternoon.

SATURDAY 12.45

Less than twenty-four hours to go.

Tomorrow, some 1,500 people will fill this building and with one voice affirm their wish to see us ordained. Now, outside in the streets is a medieval fair celebrating the 600th anniversary of the Cathedral School. Musicians in medieval dress stroll among the gardens. There is maypole dancing, street theatre, a bull being paraded up and down, a Punch and Judy show, a scribe penning testimonials, gas-filled balloons, and stalls selling sweets and crafts of various kinds. The Bishop in his purple cassock chats with people and takes photographs.

5.15

These are now my last minutes in the chapel before I go to Evensong – after which the cathedral will be closed until tomorrow. What have these last minutes to say? What has this chapel of the Mother and Child to say to me, over and above the deep comfort it has given?

Laurence Reading arrives and I thank him for all his support.

In the evening after dinner we have what is called the Bishop's Charge. The Trollopian facade is suddenly dropped and behind it we have a very real sense of the man of prayer that is John Eastaugh.

"You are called," he says, "not to do a job but to live a life." He stresses the importance of learning to wait and quotes "Go to Jerusalem and wait there for the Holy Spirit."

He continues, "From tomorrow your lives will be different. You will be leaping into a void. Until you have made the leap you cannot know what sacrifices and demands will be asked of you. You cannot turn back. Before, life was easier, your own. But in the void are God's arms and you will be leaping into them. He will never ask of you anything for which He has not prepared you and for which he will not give you the strength."

SUNDAY JUNE 28TH

Last night I had the most appalling nightmares of being trapped in violent, bloody, dangerous situations; death the only way out!

This morning we all say Matins together in the Bishop's private chapel and then walk in his garden. I do a slow walking meditation, step by step, aware of every branch, leaf, flower and stone. The bell rings for breakfast and I'm tempted not to go but, rather than appear singular, I follow the others in.

Now as we wait, we hear people arriving and the building sounds like the humming of bees inside a vast hive. We assemble, two by two, outside the great doors, with the Bishop, the Dean, the Archdeacon of Ludlow – all of them in splendid copes – and Laurence Reading, bearded and tall, with his long El Greco face and beard, looking like a Byzantine saint, plus all the other clergy, as well as the Apparitor and Registrar in his legal wig and black gown.

The doors open and we hear the voices of that vast gathering singing the first hymn. We are all nervous. We move forward to join the long procession up the nave and then, as we turn into our pews, I see Hywel, and Meinrad and other friends.

Then comes the moment. As I step forward and kneel down in front of the Bishop it feels as if I am being buried alive in a cave of darkness as his hands press down firmly on my head, and the hands of some fifty clergy also hover over me. It is as though I'm being pushed down under the waters of this new baptism, a kind of death. Then, as the cloud of hands withdraws, I am released and step back, shaking and shivering. Now the cloud is moving in again for the next candidate, followed by the same solemn and unwavering words of consecration.

Each of us then moves out to give a kiss of peace to our own families and friends, after which we gather round the altar to take part in the consecration of the bread and wine. Each of us then takes a ciborium containing the Eucharistic wafers to the faithful, these long queues stretching the whole length of the nave. Suddenly, in front of me, his face shining with so much joy, is Brother David, then Brother Alban, Hywel, Meinrad, my agent Bruce Hunter, and others: so many faces looking up into mine as I make the sign of the cross with the wafer, then lower it into the upraised hand of each, holding their gaze.

Meinrad drives me back to the Old Rectory – Hywel and the others have gone ahead to organise everything – and on the way we stop at the Carmelite monastery in Presteigne where Sister Clare comes out to greet me. "Be a good priest!" she says.

At the Old Rectory, Bishop Bill, Brother David, Brother Alban and other friars and friends are already in the garden having a picnic lunch. House and garden are alive with the presence of many friends, and suddenly, looking up, I see the buzzards soaring high above, circling the valley. Then, suddenly, it is four o'clock and we crowd into the cellar chapel to celebrate my first Eucharist.

JULY 7TH

The first rehearsal of my adaptation of Helen Hanff's *84 Charing Cross Road* at the Salisbury Playhouse. In the large rehearsal room the set is all marked out, with all the props on hand and several of the key pieces of furniture.

JULY 31ST

84 has opened! Splendid reviews in the *Times*, the *Telegraph*, and the *Financial Times*. Hywel and I drive to Wales in a terrific storm to find the garden overgrown after six weeks of neglect.

JUNE 29TH

Early in the morning I am rung up by the *Guardian*. It so happens that yesterday Tim Beaumont (Lord Beaumont of Whitley, the Liberal peer) was in Hereford on Liberal party business, and attended the early Eucharist in the cathedral when the names of those to be ordained were read out. Hearing my name he rang a journalist and said, "Did you know that James Roose-Evans is being ordained?" For, up to now, only twelve people knew.

The *Guardian* want to run a story about the first British theatre director to be ordained and still continue working in the theatre. I reply that I would prefer to have no publicity since I have yet to learn how to keep the two roles in tandem. To my delight, the *Guardian* agrees not to pursue the matter.

AUGUST 8TH

Work in the garden continues: pruning, mowing, weeding. News arrives that we have had one Broadway offer for my production of *84*, and four West End offers!

While Hywel goes off to get paving stones for the path, I foolishly take the ladder up the lane to saw off a high overhanging branch. The ladder bounces and I narrowly miss falling on my back. Hywel, on his return, rightly rebukes me.

In the evening, in the deepening dusk, we lie, tired and content, on the swing hammock, under its arbour of honeysuckle and roses, the wind blowing at the silhouettes of trees and hedges.

AUGUST 9TH

The church is to be set up for a concert by the York Winds of Toronto. Because the Peter Eugene Ball exhibition of sculpture is still in place, we arrange for the musicians to play in the centre of the nave, with the audience ranged all round them. After Samuel Barber's *Music for a Summer Night* everyone emerges, faces glowing, to drink wine and stroll among the graves.

The musicians respond to the warmth and alertness of the audience and afterwards, walking back with them to the Old Rectory, Diana Walker tells them, "The church probably wouldn't be here if it weren't for James" – as a result of which they insist on taking neither a fee nor anything for expenses.

August 12th

To Plas Newydd for the event I've been working on for over a year – the Victorian Extravaganza, which is to be repeated there for three nights in succession.

Beryl Fogg is making herself up very credibly as Queen Victoria. The Punch and Judy man rolls up to tell us he is the fourth generation of puppeteers. Then the man from Paine's fireworks appears to inform us that the floating platform on the Menai Strait, from which the fireworks are to be launched, is no good and will sink with all his equipment. Warren Davies begins to set out the Calor gas floodlights and I suggest that all the windows of the stately home should be lit from within as they would have been for Queen Victoria had she been staying there.

Already by seven o'clock it looks like a huge garden party from *The Pallisers*. There are carriage rides with the horses trotting swiftly; a Victorian cricket match is in progress; a huge hot air balloon is released with a flame roaring inside; tutu'd fairies flit in and out of trees and bushes; a stilt walker in a death's head mask sends the dogs barking. There are fish stalls, sweet stalls, hot potato stalls and flower sellers, while a young harpist sits playing Welsh folk songs under the trees. To our delight most of the public, even whole families, are dressed in Victorian costume!

There is constant movement and bustle, everything working according to plan and then, at last, everyone lines the route for the arrival of the Queen in an open Landau. Trumpeters appear on the battlements to play a royal fanfare as Her Majesty passes under a giant arch of evergreen with the word "VICTORIA" picked out in bright flowers.

As it grows dark a fire-eater leaps up onto the cromlech and people gather round these ancient stones to watch. Hundreds of them walk with hand-held flares to the banks of the Menai Strait to hear the orchestra play Handel's *Fireworks*. Sky rockets explode, their starry trails reflected in the water. Finally, some two thousand people turn with their flares to see the tiny figure of Queen Victoria high up on the floodlit balcony, speaking to them first in English and then in Welsh. A brass band strikes up and a male voice choir breaks into tune, with all that vast gathering joining in the singing of both national anthems under the night sky.

SEPTEMBER 10TH

A year ago the village school was closed and put up for auction. I have since written countless letters to try and raise the money to buy it for the Bleddfa Trust, rather than let it be converted into a bungalow. We now have a fund of £15,000. And so I set off to the auction with the agent who is to do the bidding on our behalf. There is only one other bidder, a woman with her daughter, who obviously have their eyes on converting it into a private dwelling. The woman finally stops at £14,000 – so the Trust becomes the owner of the building!

SEPTEMBER 11TH

Now more letters have to be written to raise further funding to convert it into *The Old School Gallery*! I set to …

SEPTEMBER 13TH

Diana Walker gives me a healing session and as her hands rest on me at the end I hear inwardly the words, "You don't have to carry all the burden. Others are coming to help you."

SEPTEMBER 15TH

Hywel and I are invited to dinner with Brandon and Flavia Cadbury. Afterwards he hands me a cheque for the Bleddfa Trust for £2,000, saying that more may be coming in December from his father's Trust.

SATURDAY

We have scheduled a week-end event. In the Old School, Rachel Verney and Sarah Caird speak about music therapy, while in the afternoon Margaret Hebbelthwaite speaks on the theme "The Motherhood of God".

SUNDAY

Una Kroll, deaconess, is scheduled to lead a day-long workshop in the Church. She has stayed overnight at the Old Rectory to prepare. As I go down to celebrate the Eucharist in the cellar chapel, I find her prostrate in prayer on the flagstones.

OCTOBER 10TH

At Pentecost tongues of fire descended on the assembled friends of Jesus and "everyone heard the apostles speaking in their own tongue, yet each understood the other". I realise how, increasingly, the light is breaking through unexpected cracks, through people of varying and often contrasting backgrounds, both cultural and religious, so that Christianity is not seen as sole possessor of the truth. There is nothing contradictory about this, for they are all speaking about the same divine reality.

NOVEMBER 27TH

Unanimous praise from all the critics on the opening of *84 Charing Cross Road* at the Ambassadors Theatre, and the box office telephone rings all day!

CHRISTMAS DAY

The Old Rectory. Hywel and I open our presents. I throw countless apples onto the snow for the birds but, even so, the blackbirds chase each other as though there were not enough. They advance across the snow like Napoleon's troops on Moscow, attacking the apples, hollowing them out with their beaks.

After lunch Hywel and I go for a long walk up in the hills, high up into a tundra-like waste – white fields rising to meet a white sky with mist advancing rapidly. No sheep are visible and there are no sounds other than the trickle of the stream. An owl wings its way silently across the frozen wastes.

We have tea by the fire, read, have supper; a quiet, remote, meditative, wrapped-away Christmas.

1982

A visit to the artist Thetis Blacker to discuss her forth-coming exhibition of batik banners at Bleddfa. Inside the front door of the family home is a fourteenth-century, almost life-size, statue of Christ in painted wood, riding on a donkey. Thetis tells me how recently, her mother, in her eighties, alone at home, was woken one night by a burglar who asked where she kept her money.

She replied that she didn't have any, to which he retorted, "People like you always have money!"

She replied, "And it's because of people like you that people like me keep our money in the bank!"

He then asked where she kept her jewellery, so she led him into her bedroom and showed him the safe. As she sat on the edge of the bed, watching him, she said, "You don't seem very happy in your work."

"What do you expect with the country going to the dogs!" he replied, a remark worthy of a character in one of Bernard Shaw's plays!

On the way downstairs, he told her he had cut the telephone wires; then as he passed the wooden donkey in the hall he remarked, "Lot of old religious stuff you've got here!" to which Mrs Blacker replied, "You might like to know that it is the most valuable thing in the house!"

As soon as he was gone, although it was three in the morning, she put on a coat over her dressing gown and went down the drive to knock on a neighbour's door and report the theft to the police.

March 5ᵀᴴ

At the Old Rectory I am visited by Meinrad and Rosemary, both of whom have now left Stanbrook and are living in a borrowed cottage at Eastcote near Ledbury. They arrive in Meinrad's red VW Beetle, laughing, with rainbow coloured scarves, looking like gypsies. There is much rich, good talk and we look at Meinrad's new pictures, which are like icons in their powerful glazed colours. She begins with scraper board and then uses coloured inks, putting a glaze on each as she works. Potent figures emerge out of green-black darkness, images dredged up from her unconscious.

We sit for a while in the cellar chapel.

"It is a holy space," says Rosemary. She speaks about the gentility and cleanness of so much Christian worship, especially in England and Switzerland. "There is need for holy dirt and holy muddle," she says, "as in this cellar chapel where there is the smell of earth, of stone, the sound of birds, and the very under-groundness of it."

They both speak about the monastic life that is now behind them, how it is more important "to live in wholeness" than to be slaves to a set of rules. They suggest that the masculine psyche, for which the monastic life was first designed, responds better to rules, whereas women get uptight and suffer from scruples, or become very lazy!

I recall Dom Jerome Hodkinson, Abbot at Belmont, who regularly visited the community at Stanbrook, saying the same thing. Perhaps the secret lies in small, family-sized communities, like the Carmelites.

Meinrad speaks about one nun at Stanbrook who used to smash dishes and swear and who, one day during the Ash Wednesday liturgy, stormed out of the chapel, slamming the great door of the Abbey church and shouting "Hypocrites! The lot of you!"

I comment on how this nun was the "shadow" side of the community, carrying all that was being repressed.

APRIL 3ᴿᴰ

Dinner with Douglas Evans and his wife Olwen at Dolau Garage. Douglas, who keeps an eye on my car, says how he loves visiting old churches, although he is not a church or chapel goer. "I've seen too much of what so-called Christians have done," he says. He also talks about the decline of morale in the countryside, and the greed that seems to affect everyone: "Even local people who call in at the garage don't want to talk or relate. Ever since the 1950s, after the last war, people don't seem to want to help each other as they used to."

JULY 31ST

The opening of the exhibition of Thetis Blacker's batik banners in Bleddfa church, which Hywel has organised. Thetis is overwhelmed. The banners, suspended from the beams, and skilfully lit, transform the church into a small cathedral. A large crowd of people file into the church to the sound of Javanese bells and the smell of Tibetan incense. Michael Croft of Croft Castle speaks about the visionary quality of Thetis's work. We end up taking just over £1000 in the first twenty-four hours.

AUGUST 2ND

Hywel and I drive to have tea with Michael Yeates in his hotel near Abergwesyn – a tall Georgian house with orange blinds scalloped in white, pots of lilies standing on either side of the front door, and the flag of St George fluttering from a pole above the porch. The hotel is finished like a country house, with his own books on the shelves. He and Valentine Mehun descend from their afternoon siesta and we have tea. "Welsh tea-cakes buttered on both sides for James!" orders Michael.

He tells us about Blodwyn, one of the maids in his kitchens who is often bewildered by the names of some of the rare vegetables he uses in cooking. One evening, Lady Delia Venables Llewelyn and her family were in for dinner. Michael insists that guests be on time as meals are cooked for each table. On this particular evening he was busy keeping his eye on the pots, some on the boil, some simmering, some poaching, when he suddenly said to Blodwyn, "Are the Llewelyns ready for the next course?" She thought he was referring to one of the vegetables and, lifting one lid after another, said, "Which are they?"

AUGUST 22ND

I return to London to discuss plans for the Broadway production of *84 Charing Cross Road*, which I've been asked to direct. An honour of course, but the prospect is exhausting! The past seventeen months have been unremitting grind: the tour of *Private Lives*, *84* at Salisbury and at the Ambassadors; the Victorian Extravaganza at Plas Newydd, organising the Bleddfa Trust's programme for this year, writing endless letters begging for contributions – not to mention being ordained! Plus book chapters, reviews, articles, sermons, workshops. I need a holiday – and indeed a holy day, for such deep tiredness also betokens a tiredness at one's very roots. It is true also that for some months now I have neglected the practice of meditation, that communion from which new energy can come. "The answer", as Hywel observes, "is always within."

1983

I have a massage session with the healer Hjilmar Schonauer. He works simply, quietly, by candlelight, and then suddenly, towards the end, he blows softly, clicking his fingers. At once I sense presences filling the room. Gently he covers me with a blanket, blows out the candle, and leaves me. I have sensed presences before: once on my birthday when they filled the kitchen at the Old Rectory, and once in my bedroom when the presences were flowing in through the open window and were all around me.

I think of what Tristram Beresford wrote in *A Communication*, from his book, *The Ungainsayable Presence*:

They are here now, those who have care of me.
Their love is like an ocean flowing in
To enclose an island.

Lying there in the dark in that small cell-like room I sense them now and hear them saying, "Yield. Come with us." And I know that they are at work, kneading and changing me. They have been there a long time in the background, waiting, and I have resisted them and not listened. But that is perhaps why I now have all these aches and pains: how else to deal with so stubborn and wilful a person?

I know that I have to return to the practice of meditation, which I have neglected of late, and that it must take a new form: listening, letting go, waiting; not even using a mantra – for too often in the past I have consciously held on to the mantra. I must learn just to be, to wait in silence.

On his return Hjilmar talks gently. That large, sad, humorous face. He feels that my pains signal changes, that I am en route to being and owning myself, making my own choices rather than inherited ones.

MAY 12TH

To an auction at Castell Madoc, Upper Chapel, beyond Builth Wells. The house is dark and rambling, set in a neglected garden. There are rows of tables arrayed with china and glass, while from the open windows of the house pictures and other objects are held up to view by the auctioneer. On the inner lawn are various items of furniture.

We bump into Ed Paynes, an artist, gaunt and grey-bearded, looking like Ben Gunn in *Treasure Island*. I mention to him that I'm interested in a mahogany towel rail. People push in and around and the bidding goes so fast that I don't even attempt to make a bid for it. Then I see Ed, his eyes excited, as he starts bidding. The bidding stops at £30 and I say to Hywel, "Oh, I'm so glad Ed has got it. Clearly he wanted it!" Ed comes up to us and excitedly pushes £5 into my hand saying, "I bought it for you, but I knew you didn't want to go over £25, so the £5 is from me!"

We try to return the money to him, knowing he is hard up. We then climb a flight of steps to an overgrown kitchen garden where there are two large lead urns, painted a dull red.

"Now, if those had been for sale," I say, "I would have bid for them."

Ed goes to pick one up.

"It will be very easy to walk off with them," he says.

"I couldn't," I reply. "I would have scruples."

"I wouldn't!" he replies.

A little later we catch sight of him moving his car to a group of trees and we realise he is going to try and take the urns. Sitting in our car we see his tall figure staggering with one urn covered over by his coat, and loading it into his car. We watch him load the second and then, waving goodbye, we drive away. He catches up with us in Builth Wells, waving frantically to us to stop.

"I took them for you!" he says, his face moist with sweat.

"But we don't want them, Ed, really!" we protest.

"Well, there's gratitude for you!" he sulks and so, to avoid a scene, we load them into our boot.

Back as the Old Rectory we continue to feel ill at ease and so we decide to return them. Two nights later, when there is no moon, we drive back and, after switching off the lights, dump the urns by the gates and return home, feeling much relieved!

May 17ᵀᴴ

Today I spoke at the Deanery meeting at the request of Geoffrey Asson, vicar of Kington, to whose parish I am assigned as one of the team. My priest friend John Hencher had warned me against speaking to fellow clergy. How right he was! I spoke briefly about the work of the Bleddfa Trust and then invited questions. Anthony Perry, vicar of Presteigne, asked why the Deanery had not been consulted about the dates of various retreats we have arranged. I pointed out that as Bleddfa is in Wales and not England we have no obligation to the clergy of the Hereford diocese, but also that we are not a church-based organisation. Then the youngest clergyman present, who arrived in black leathers on a motorbike, and who has never been to Bleddfa, accused us of being "exotic and unreal, suitable only for young women in long dresses, doing yoga and eating yoghurt. Why aren't you doing something about lowering the price of land?"

I reply by suggesting that since Saint Paul says we all have different gifts he could concentrate on lowering the price of land while I concentrate on stretching peoples minds and imaginations!

Mercifully I side-step a dangerous question: "What comments have you to make of the church and its sti-pendiary ministry?" I reply by saying I have no wish to be martyred and so decline to answer! But the whole experience has left me feeling shattered. When I report all this back to John Hencher he says, "James I warned you! I told you to stay away!"

1985

I visit Kathleen Lomax in her black and white cottage at Nash, outside Presteigne. She has arthritis in hands, feet and neck, as well as Parkinson's, yet still lives on her own. When I ask her what she has been doing she tells me that all the plums she has picked have been skinned and bottled, while all her pears have been placed in trays so that when they are ripe she can bottle them also.

Since she can only move by putting one foot in front of the other, unable to look to left or right without stopping and shuffling her whole body round, everything takes much longer to accomplish. No wonder neighbours were relieved when she stopped driving, for she could only drive in third gear, at 30 mph, and was unable to look round! Yet she persists in entertaining friends to lunch, and will take no shortcuts: everything has to be just so – the table laid with a cloth and mats, napkins in rings, the best cutlery and china (the plates already warmed) and with a choice of two or three vegetables for the main course.

She hoards everything in an extraordinarily methodical manner: paper bags fastened together and hung on a peg, small tins filled with elastic bands, neat collections of string, paperclips, polythene bags ... And she knows where everything is.

After lunch she sits in her favourite chair. She has developed a special technique for sitting down. Standing in front of a chair, she then falls back into it, so that her legs swing up onto the pouf in front. Once there, her head, with its Eton crop of white hair, rests against the back of the chair. There is a fixity about her conversation caused by the physical inability to move her head, which sometimes she asks me to massage.

She has such a lively interest in everyone and every-thing, reading at least two books a week, and yet she can also be silent. We are often very happy just sitting there, saying nothing. She calls me Humph (having discovered my second name is Humphrey) and says, "Dear Humph, don't let anyone else call you by that name."

As I leave she kisses me goodbye, saying, "It is so long since I have been loved and had anyone to love." And I know that our friendship has been the last gift of her life.

MARCH 3RD

Dr John Goodall-Copestake rings to tell me Kathleen has suffered major bleeding and been taken to hospital. I drive over to give her holy communion and to anoint her. The doctor says her kidneys have packed up and that it is a matter of days.

MARCH 4TH

I tell the congregation at Knill that Kathleen is dying and

that for her funeral the church should be decorated with autumn branches, as for a harvest festival, with apples from her own store, and the bottled plums she has done, all neatly labelled in her own hand. Her funeral, I say, should be like a harvest festival: a celebration of her life.

TUESDAY MORNING

The hospital rings me at five am. I dress quickly and drive into Hereford, with Venus low on the horizon, expecting that Kathleen may go at any moment. I stay with her in a side room for ten hours, as they give her injections. In the afternoon they remove the drip. An oxygen mask is placed over her mouth and at intervals the nurses give her sips of water. Her eyes are always open, concentrating on her breathing, as though all her energy is focused on that. At one point, as her eyes clear and I lean in close to her, she gazes contentedly into my face for several minutes. The nurses gently wash and turn her. I meditate and say some prayers. I hold her hand, knowing that other presences are assembling to assist her.

I return to Bleddfa to get some sleep and then at seven twenty the nurse rings to say, "Father, this is just to let you know that Miss Lomax has gone."

MARCH 16TH

We prepare for the funeral.

I go to Kathleen's cottage with Mrs Thomas, who cleaned for her, and from the garage take down the trays of pears and apples to carry over to the church. As we lift one tray I notice shredded newspaper and that some of the apples have been eaten. Suddenly a mouse jumps out and I yelp, which makes Mrs Thomas laugh.

Everyone helps to decorate the church and I place the boxes of pears and apples in the window bays, and the bottled plums on the pulpit and font, as well as two samples of books she had bound in leather. The whole church looks as festive as for a harvest festival, which is what I had planned.

Knill is on the outskirts of Presteigne, a small town often referred to as one of the gateways to Wales. It has a handsome medieval church, and the Judge's Lodgings, the latter being the former Shire Hall. Apart from its local community it seems always to have attracted writers, musicians and artists, as well as colourful characters of whom the most outstanding is Rhoda Partridge. On her daily progress of the town on her two mile walk, now in her eighties, splendidly dressed, and carrying a Gandalfian stick, she stops to greet each person she meets and engages in conversation. To each she listens, but never gossips. She is the recipient of many confidences and widely trusted.

When young she married a successful farmer and brought up six children. Then, at the age of forty, she decided she wanted to learn to fly a glider and so, first, she trained as a potter and became a successful ceramicist. This enabled her to afford to learn to glide and then buy her own glider. She also wrote a regular column on gliding for a German publication, which enabled her to buy the latest model every three years at a discount because of the publicity she gave it in her column. She always referred to her glider as "my broomstick". In her early gliding days she soared to heights no other woman pilot had before achieved. She even flew the glider over the Alps. On one memorable occasion she persuaded the pilot of a Jumbo jet to let her take over the controls. He turned to her and said, "Mrs Partridge, have you ever flown a plane before?" And she replied, "Oh, only a glider, low-level flying you know!"

I once received a letter from her that began, "Darling James, dear James, good James, sweet James…" I thought: this is the biggest flirt in Radnorshire! But what can one expect when you learn that at the age of fifteen, staying with her grandmother in Venice, she was driven regularly by Westbrook, her grandmother's dignified chauffeur, to be taught to dance by gigolos at the Casino in Cannes! "Remind me," said Rhoda one day, "to tell you what happened when my knickers came down during a Viennese waltz!"

The stories about her are legendary while the tale of how she came to live in Presteigne is now part of the town's history. It is the story of a goddess who one day, flying above the clouds, suddenly saw the clouds opening in a circular formation to reveal a small town nestling below.

"There," said the goddess, looking down from a glider, "is where I shall come to earth and live among mortals!"

The next day she drove into Presteigne and bought her

house off the main street. It was 1976 and she at once enrolled at the Hereford College of Art on a four year course to study fine art, drawing and etching. Later she was to learn to paint watercolours, and make willow sculpture, holding one exhibition after another. She is constantly questioning and exploring. Whenever I think of her I am reminded of George Herbert's line, "In age I bud again."

Afterword

However far I travel, it is to this place that I return like a homing bird. Amazingly, this border country of Wales is still largely unspoilt. As Peter Conradi observes in *At the Bright Hem of God*: "I did not think that I had ever visited a place of such transcendent magic. Here were sublime views over the ancient hills, the shock of silence, and then the surprise of a new feeling compounded of exhilaration, trust and peace of mind."

One may walk for an entire day, or drive one's car up narrow winding lanes into the hills, and not see another vehicle or person. Kilvert would recognise this landscape, and indeed, when I give readings of his Clyro diaries in some of the small remote churches of Radnorshire, it is as though his spirit is still with us.

The one thing Kilvert would miss would be the intricate network of railway lines that brought steam trains to such places as Titley, Presteigne, Hay and many more. Today those lines are mainly overgrown, although on special occasions a steam train can be seen puffing into Knighton Station on a day excursion. The novelist, Sue Gee, writing in *Hortus* about the garden at Titley Mill, describes how "occasionally you also hear a steam train: the station and the track have been restored, and the whistle and the puff of an engine running through the nearby woods add to the atmosphere of an unworldly place". It is in Sue's haunting novel, *The Mysteries of Glass*, set in this part of the world in the 1860s, that she recreates the time when this train ran regularly to Lyonshall.

It is little wonder, as Peter Conradi observes, that so many writers through the centuries have been inspired by Radnorshire: Gerald of Wales, George Herbert, Thomas Traherne, Henry Vaughan, Francis Kilvert, Eric Gill, David Jones, Bruce Chatwin, Ruth Bidgood, and many more, including Conradi himself who, like me, has lived here for more than forty years. And not just writers. Today many musicians, artists, writers, sculptors also make their home here.

One of my favourite walks is on Stonewall Hill, between Presteigne and Knighton. There are buzzards and even occasionally a red kite. And if one stops to listen and then look up, there, high, high in the sky, is a small black dot. It is a skylark. How vividly Vaughan Williams catches, in the closing bars of his *Lark Ascending*, that quality of hovering ecstasy. At such moments it is as though, in Shakespeare's words, "the lark at Heaven's gate sings" and the world takes on a different perspective. All distractions fall away and, as in Gerard Manley Hopkins' poem, we see the "landscape plotted and pieced". Everything falls into place and we know what we must do.

As a wise woman once said to me, "When you feel down, look at a bird flying above you. Take off occasionally with strong pinions. Go above things and look down with better perspective. Think pinions, James. Think pinions!"

A note about the
Bleddfa Centre for the
Creative Spirit

The Bleddfa Centre is a place where the big questions of life are asked.

Neil McGregor, former Director of the British Museum

Bleddfa is a place where people, ideas and imaginings meet at depth, in a way that is very rare. I think it represents all that is most hopeful for our anxious and fragmented culture.

Rowan Williams, former Archbishop of Canterbury

To share with others has always been central to the vision of the Bleddfa Trust. Its work deepens the quality of life, living as we do in such a materialistic age. It stands for nourishment and healing, for the inner life of people. It is a place for celebration.

Hywel Jones, co-founder

In 1983 came the opportunity to buy Bleddfa village school, which had been closed by the local authority. With its closure the village seemed to have died: parents no longer gathered to deliver or collect their children or gossip in the little shop. I was determined, therefore, that it should remain a public building, drawing people to the community, and not be converted into a bungalow. I sat down to write hundreds of letters and having raised £15,000 I was able to purchase the school for the Bleddfa Trust. Then, aided by various grants, the building was converted into a gallery, tea rooms and shop, with a landscaped garden made possible by a grant from the Prince of Wales Trust, and the building was opened as the official Centre for Caring and the Arts by the Marchioness of Anglesey.

A few years later some adjoining land and two tumble-down barns and an orchard came on the market. Thanks to three individuals in particular: Cynthia Charlesworth, Wendy Hall and Marie Mathias, as well as a grant from the Foundation for Sport and the Arts, which Dr Miriam Stoppard secured for us, Bleddfa now has a handsome Shaker-like Barn Centre which comprises a large studio, a reception area, and small meditation chapel, built around a central courtyard with a fountain.

To mark the millennium, £30,000 was raised to commission a statue of Tobias and the Angel by the Irish sculptor Ken Thompson, which was unveiled by Dr Rowan Williams, then Archbishop of Wales and the Centre's chief patron. The Bleddfa annual lecture was also inaugurated, with its first speakers including Neil McGregor, Peter Maxwell Davies, Jonathan Porritt, Melvyn Bragg, Libby Purves and Mark Tully.

In all the ebb and flow of fortunes that the Bleddfa Centre for the Creative Spirit (as it is now named) has experienced since 1974, it has continued to explore the relationship between art and life, between the creative and the spiritual. For I believe that the majority of people possess, no matter how unused, real creative and imaginative faculties, so that the question is less one of educating people to appreciate the fine arts than of providing facilities and an environment in which they can explore and express their own creativity.

In the Barn Centre are some words by the Spanish poet and playwright Federico García Lorca, painted on wood by the calligrapher John Hencher:

The poem, the song, the picture
Is only water
Drawn from the well of the people
And it should be given back to them in a cup of
beauty
So that they may drink
And in drinking
Understand themselves.

These words sum up for me what the Centre represents. I believe that every aspect of one's life, from washing dishes, preparing a meal, digging in the garden, collecting a child from school, or helping a neighbour, can be an opportunity for being creative, for creativity is simply making something with love, and this can be expressed in so many ways. Life itself is the greatest of all arts.

Acknowledgements

This book is dedicated to those many who helped the Bleddfa Centre to grow over more than half a century. The vision and commitment of my partner Hywel Jones was decisive, as was the dedication of John Cupper who developed The Old School Gallery, and his partner John Hencher, who not only led a series of workshops but did much of the calligraphy for a number of the exhibitions. From the outset Jean and Albert Thomas were stalwart and indefatigable supporters, along with Canon Laurence Reading, Diana Walker, Fred Averis, Caroline Gourlay, and Dennis and Irene Vickers. Brandon and Flavia Cadbury, the Marquess and Marchioness of Anglesey, the Right Reverend Dr Rowan Williams, Lord Carlile of Berriew and Bronwen, Viscountess Astor kindly agreed to be our patrons. To all of the above I give heartfelt thanks.

So much is also owed to: Brian Angel, Graham and Ann Arnold and the Brotherhood of Ruralists, Joan Baker, Peter Eugene Ball, Bob Bates, Gillian Bell-Richards, Elinor Bennett, Tristram Beresford, Peter Birrel, Thetis Blacker, Sally Boyce, Hazel Bradley, Michael Buckley, Peter Burman, Sarah Verney Caird, Dame Frances Campbell-Preston, Roger Capps, Cynthia Charlesworth, David Cohen CBE, Elizabeth Cohen, Veronica Cohen, Stephanie Cole, Nicholas Colloff, Peter Conradi, Lord

Croft, Dr Brian Davies, Peter Dean, Nigel and Frances Dees, Lee Donald and Wendy Smith, Ossian Ellis, Shirley Elwell, Malcolm Forbes, Colin Francis, Michael Fraser, Ursula Freeman, Jane Gallagher, Marcia Gibson-Watt, Christopher Good, Janet Goodridge, Leon Goosens, Armand Gwynne, Wendy Hall, Bill Harper, Michael Harvey, Margaret Hebblethwaite, Belinda and Jenny Holland, Elizabeth Lady Holland, Phil Jennings, Penny Keith, Rev Bill Kirkpatrick and the Laing Trust, Jane Knott, Una Kroll, Richard Lewis, Hans and Beryl Lichtenstein, Daphne Lightfoot, Richard Livesey MP, Ishbel Macgregor, John and Judy Malleson, Marie Mathias, Chrissie McEvoy, Rev Richard McLaren, Edward Milford, Rafi Mohamed, Gareth and Angela Morgan, Richard Morgan, Margaret Morris, Tony Morris, Jim O'Neill, Mirabel Osler, George Pace, Ray Pahl, Rhoda Partridge, Jenny Pearson, Hugo Perks, John Petts, Myfanwy Pugh, Kathleen Raine, Joan Ray, Tom and Celia Read, Elizabeth Reynolds (maker of fabulous cakes!), Alexander Robertson, Rob and Moira Rowe, John Rowlands Pritchard, Caroline Sanderson, Bruno Schrecker, Dr Miriam Stoppard, Robin Tanner, John Thaw, Ken Thompson, Sir George Trevelyan, Graham Trew, Esther de Waal, Rev Victor de Waal, Islwyn and Fay Watkins, David Wheeler, Eve Wright – and many more!

James writes a fortnightly blog of thoughts and inspirations:

www.jamesrooseevans.co.uk

For information about
The Bleddfa Centre for the Creative Spirit
see:

www.bleddfacentre.org

.

Printed in Great Britain
by Amazon